GREAT LIVES OBSERVED

Gerald Emanuel Stearn, *General Editor*

EACH VOLUME IN THE SERIES VIEWS THE CHARACTER AND
ACHIEVEMENT OF A GREAT WORLD FIGURE IN THREE PER-
SPECTIVES—THROUGH HIS OWN WORDS, THROUGH THE OPIN-
IONS OF HIS CONTEMPORARIES, AND THROUGH RETROSPEC-
TIVE JUDGMENTS—THUS COMBINING THE INTIMACY OF AUTO-
BIOGRAPHY, THE IMMEDIACY OF EYEWITNESS OBSERVATION,
AND THE OBJECTIVITY OF MODERN SCHOLARSHIP.

MARGARET L. COIT, *editor of this volume in the Great Lives
Observed series, is Associate Professor of Social Science at Fairleigh Dickinson University. She was awarded the Pulitzer Prize
for Biography in 1950 for* John C. Calhoun: American Portrait.

GREAT LIVES OBSERVED

JOHN C. CALHOUN

GREAT LIVES OBSERVED

JOHN C.
Calhoun

Edited by Margaret L. Coit

The whole South is the grave of Calhoun.
—YANKEE SOLDIER (1865)

PRENTICE-HALL, INC., ENGLEWOOD CLIFFS, N.J.

Current printing (last number): 10 9 8 7 6 5 4 3 2 1

C–13–112409–9

P–13–112391–2

Library of Congress Catalog Card Number: 72–104843

Printed in the United States of America

PRENTICE-HALL INTERNATIONAL, INC. (*London*)
PRENTICE-HALL OF AUSTRALIA, PTY. LTD. (*Sydney*)
PRENTICE-HALL OF CANADA, LTD. (*Toronto*)
PRENTICE-HALL OF INDIA PRIVATE LIMITED (*New Delhi*)
PRENTICE-HALL OF JAPAN, INC. (*Tokyo*)

Contents

Acknowledgments

For assistance and advice in the preparation of this manuscript, I wish to express my thanks to Mrs. Pringle Haigh of the Charleston, South Carolina, Library Society, to Dr. W. Edwin Hemphill, editor of *The Papers of John C. Calhoun,* to Mr. E. L. Inabinett, Director of The South Caroliniana Library, to Professor Donald Johnson of New York University, to Professor Thomas R. Marmor of The University of Wisconsin, to Professor Benjamin Quarles of Morgan State College, to Mr. Robert Stanbury, formerly of the Fairleigh Dickinson University Library, and to Dr. Charles M. Wiltse, editor of *The Papers of Daniel Webster.* I also wish to thank the Fairleigh Dickinson University library staff for their constant assistance, and special thanks go to my editor, Gerald Stearn, and to Professor William Freehling of the University of Michigan, who read and criticized this manuscript in its entirety.

I hold the duties of life to be greater than life itself, and that in performing them, even against hope, our labor is not lost. I regard this life very much as a struggle against evil, and that to him who acts on proper principle, the reward is in the struggle more than in victory itself.

—JOHN C. CALHOUN

Introduction

John C. Calhoun has been called "the Hamlet and the fire-eater of the Southern cause," and his life, "a Greek tragedy in five acts." This most controversial of Southern statesmen was born on March 18, 1782, in the South Carolina up-country near Abbeville, in what is now Anderson County. Then it was the old District of Ninety-Six, the Long Canes country, on the edge of the open frontier. Here, in the rolling red hills, the last echoes of the Revolution were sounding. The leader of the community was a surveyor, a hard-bitten Revolutionary veteran and Indian fighter named Patrick Calhoun. He was fifty-four when his third son was born to his young wife, Martha Caldwell, a dark-haired, "tall, stately" woman of Lowland Scottish origins.

In 1733 when he was five, Patrick Calhoun had come with his family to the United States from the beautiful mountain country of Donegal, Ireland. Landing in Philadelphia, the Calhouns had followed the line of the frontier southwards from old Fort Duquesne to the Waxhaws and then westward, almost to the mountains. There, for a generation, they helped hold off the Indians. They survived the Long Cane massacre of 1760 when Patrick's mother was "most inhumanly butchered," and two young nieces were seized and taken into captivity by the Cherokees. Years of troubled peace followed, with Patrick and other "Regulators" continually patrolling the frontier. There Patrick organized a church in the wilderness and built the first frame house in the community. Later, he was to bring in the first slaves. In 1769 "Pat" Calhoun led his neighbors two hundred miles on foot to a polling place near Charleston where at gunpoint they seized the ballot and elected him to the South Carolina State Legislature.

Young John Caldwell Calhoun grew up to a heritage of politics and of battle. In the flickering firelight, clamped between his father's knees, he heard stories of Indian atrocities, of Tory barbarities, of the uncle who fell at Cowpens, and the uncle, Major John Caldwell, who was cut down by the "Bloody Scout" in his own yard. Patrick had battled against adoption of the United States Constitution, because it permitted taxation of South Carolinians. That government was best, he would say, which governed least, throwing off all "needless restraints," and allowing the individual the most freedom "compatible

1

with order and tranquillity." This Jeffersonian doctrine was absorbed by young John Calhoun.

John C. Calhoun had little early education. He attended a log cabin "old field school," where he learned his letters, and he dove into the books his father brought home; by the time he was thirteen he had memorized passages in Thomas Paine's *The Rights of Man.* For a brief period, he was given the run of his brother-in-law Moses Waddell's classical and historical library, where he read until his health gave out. His sister had died; his father was dying, and John was sent home to the lonely Long Cane country to manage the family farm and to grow up like Lincoln in utter intellectual solitude. When he was eighteen an astounded passer-by saw John out plowing with a book tied to the plow! The neighbors concluded that John C. Calhoun should be educated, and his two older brothers were sent for.

But John himself hesitated. The peace and beauty of the southern farm life had gone deep into him; out of his love for the land would come all his future political thinking. He was a planter and content to be a planter. He was convinced that half an education would be worse than none; he would settle for nothing less than the best education the young United States had to offer.

The family council agreed. The young man was sent to Moses Waddell's famed "log college," where for two years he absorbed his Latin and Greek and made up for the deficiencies of his early schooling. In 1802 he entered the junior class at Yale University.

Calhoun stood out as a rebel at Yale. He was a brilliant student. He "made" Phi Beta Kappa in time to hear a debate on whether or not a division of the Union would be "politick." But he refused to join the Church of Christ or the Moral Society and he refused to accept any doctrines that he could not see the practical value of. Worst of all, in Federalist New England, he was an avowed Jefferson Republican. It is said that the President of Yale, Timothy Dwight, predicted that Calhoun would some day be President of the United States; it is known that he drove himself so relentlessly because he intended to become a member of Congress—and soon. Graduating with honors, he was assigned a commencement oration, "The Qualities Necessary to Make a Statesman."

From Yale he entered Tapping Reeve's great law school in Litchfield, Connecticut, where he studied for two years. He spent his vacations in Newport, Rhode Island, with Calhoun cousins from Charleston. Early in 1811, he married his second cousin, Floride, when she was nineteen and he was nearly twenty-nine years old.

He completed his law studies in Charleston (a city that he dismissed as "corrupt"), opened an office in Abbeville, and won his first public acclaim by eloquently presenting resolutions of indignation against an attack by the British ship, the *Leopard,* upon the American frigate, *Chesapeake.* In 1807, a tall, intense young man with shaggy hair and brilliant dark eyes, John C. Calhoun was elected without opposition to the legislative seat long held by his father. A leader of the House soon predicted that they would find "this long gawky fellow from Abbeville hard to manage."

During Calhoun's legislative service the state was redistricted, giving the two great "interests," the coastal plains and the back country, protection against one another. Calhoun described this later as an example of the "concurrent majority," which was to become his hallmark, "not of one portion of the people over another portion." The future political philosopher would dramatize how deeply this particular lesson had sunk into him.

Late in 1810 Calhoun was swept into Congress in the tidal wave of young frontiersmen from the West and South which engulfed Washington and hurled the country into war. As one of the fervent "War-Hawks" of 1812, Calhoun was second-in-command to that "clever man," the "Western Star," the thirty-five-year-old Speaker, Henry Clay. It was Calhoun who submitted the Foreign Relations Committee Report, calling for fifty thousand volunteers and the arming of ships for war with England. It was Calhoun who took on the erratic, brilliant John Randolph of Roanoke. Randolph saw the conflict as global, with England standing alone against Napoleon, the arch-enemy of mankind. But Calhoun scorned any "tame submission to wrongs." Our seamen had been impressed by Britain, our ships sunk. It was the duty of the government to "protect every citizen in the lawful pursuit of his business. . . . Protection and patriotism are reciprocal." This would be a war of defense, not aggression, the defense of "violated rights." A young Richmond editor early recognized the young Calhoun as "one of the master spirits, who stamp their names upon the age in which they live." To Thomas Ritchie, Calhoun seemed "like one of the sages of the old Congress with all the graces of youth."

During the subsequent thirty months of the war, Calhoun in "ringing" speeches, sometimes read aloud to the troops, pressed the cause, pitted hope against hopelessness, and battled unsuccessfully for military conscription. He ran into bitter opposition from the New Hampshire Congressman, Daniel Webster, who thought that the New England states might "interpose between their citizens and arbitrary power." But Calhoun answered that a minority had no "right to involve the country in ruin." In the darkest hours of the conflict he held firm. Later he was said to be "the young Hercules who had borne the war upon his shoulders."

Few failed to feel the force and fire within him. In peace as in war, he dominated the House, and although "not eloquent," was an intense and lucid orator. He and Henry Clay and the other "War-Hawks" now advocated nationalist programs for an expanding America. "The greatest of all calamities," Calhoun saw as "next to the loss of liberty —disunion." The very word, he said, comprehended "almost the sum of our political dangers, and against it . . . we ought to be perpetually guarded."

Calhoun had been aware from the first of the danger of Southern nationalism. As early as 1812 he had foreseen that when the South felt its liberties threatened, when it no longer controlled the Union, it would resort to seceding from the Union. He therefore dedicated himself to a lifelong struggle against any force or forces that would rend the Union apart. For him, as for Daniel Webster years later, liberty and union were inseparable. We are charged by Providence, he told the House, "not only with the happiness of this great people but with that of the human race. We have a government of a new order . . . founded on the rights of man, resting on . . . reason."

He spoke for a national bank to regulate the wildcat paper money loose across the land. He called for "great roads" and canals, not only for defense, but to bind together the sections and the interests of "this great country," to "conquer space." Distances, he thought, strained the sympathies of our nature. Thus he supported a moderate protective tariff, "not for South Carolina but for the nation" because he was aware that American textiles were facing stringent foreign competition and he felt that the tariff would bring harmony to the diverse interests of the country. The tariff was of no benefit to South Carolina; but it was not injurious to South Carolina and thereby to the general welfare, or to "justice" which Calhoun saw as the primary objective of government. He was, as young Webster was, a sectionalist and a nationalist at the same time, and each demanded protection for his immediate constituency when he felt it to be endangered.

Still young and keenly ambitious, Calhoun shouldered a major challenge when in December, 1817, he took over as President James Monroe's Secretary of War. The post had been previously rejected by Andrew Jackson, Henry Clay, Langdon Cheves, and William Lowndes; Calhoun's friends feared that his "brilliant powers" would be buried under the details of executive routine. Instead, Calhoun brought luster to the office, ironically helping build it to a strength that enabled it to withstand the test of the Civil War.

West Point was one of Calhoun's primary concerns; among the cadets he appointed were Robert E. Lee, Joseph Johnson, and Jefferson Davis. He developed a program for integrating the Indians into the mainstream of American life and, as a member of Monroe's cabinet, was a participant in the great debates over the Missouri Compromise, the Monroe Doctrine, and General Andrew Jackson's unauthorized military vendetta into Spanish Florida. In several instances in later years, Calhoun's conclusions would rise to haunt him.

At forty-two he leaped into the presidential hurly-burly of 1824, but withdrew from the five-man race when it was clear that he could not win. He settled instead for the vice-presidency. Although supposedly an "Adams man," Calhoun was deeply disturbed by an alleged "bargain and corruption" deal when Adams named Clay Secretary of State. From that time on Calhoun became an avowed Jackson supporter. Adams viewed his defection with bitterness which increased when as Vice-President Calhoun permitted the half-mad John Randolph of Roanoke, now a Senator, to attack the President venomously.

But Calhoun, as his private correspondence reveals, was not indulging in mere "factious opposition." He genuinely believed that the liberty of the country was in danger, and that there was good reason for "a powerful opposition to the Executive," as he wrote his friend Micah Sterling. He saw the power of the presidential office as kingly and only because it was dependent on the people could it be called democratic. If the President, or a powerful combination of henchmen, could choose his successor, "our government would no longer be a republick." The 1824 election had depended on a coalition in the House. Henry Clay, who headed it, had "been placed by the power created by his own efforts in the line of safe precedents. He has gone over from the side of the people to the side of power." [1]

Early in his career Calhoun was thus turning his brilliant mind towards what would become a primary concern of his later years: the powers and limitations of government in a democratic society, more specifically the relation of the states to the federal government. John Randolph goaded Calhoun's thinking with his interminable tirades upon the Senate floor.

Randolph had detected the fatal weakness in the Missouri Compro-

[1] Letter from Calhoun to Micah Sterling, May 31, 1826. John C. Calhoun Papers, South Caroliniana Library of the University of South Carolina.

mise: that if one acknowledged the power of Congress to limit slavery
in the territories, why not in all the new states, and eventually, why
could not slavery itself be abolished by a simple act of Congress? "We
must concern ourselves with what is and slavery exists," warned Randolph. "It is to us a question of life and death . . . a necessity imposed
upon the South, not a Utopia of our seeking." He was bidding the
South to look to its defenses. "We are the eel that is being flayed," he
shouted. Yet, despite Randolph's warnings, it was not slavery that was
under attack—not yet—but rather the "tariff humbug," which he had
comprehended back in 1816, far more clearly than had Calhoun.

Although the crippling postwar economic depression was over for
most of the country, the South remained depressed. Undoubtedly, the
overproduction of cotton was partly to blame, but this the South did
not or could not see. What it did see was that the tariff, avowedly
protective by 1824, was benefiting Northern manufacturers at the expense of Southern farmers, who, in consequence, had to pay higher
and higher prices for everything they had to buy. Calhoun saw further
—he saw a determination on the part of the North, whether consciously acknowledged or not, to reduce the South to colonial dependency.

What could be done? This was the burden of Calhoun's anguished
thought during his vice-presidential years. He wanted to be President;
whichever side he took would cost him the support of the other. The
test came with the Woolens Bill of 1827; Calhoun cast the deciding
vote—against protection.

But the tide could not be reversed. The North, Calhoun was convinced, would sacrifice the "general welfare" for financial profit; the
South was openly "calculating the value of the Union." In South
Carolina the farm depression was so acute that not even Calhoun
could sell his good cotton crop above the cost of cultivation. Soon,
fire-eaters would be threatening secession. What should Calhoun do?
What could he do?

Sleepless night after night, Calhoun paced the gallery of his home
in the Blue Ridge foothills, then came to his decision. In what was
gradually recognized as his creation, although not at first acknowledged as such, Calhoun wrote a denunciation of the tariff in the so-
called "South Carolina Exposition and Protest," later adopted by the
State Legislature. What, he asked, was the remedy against a "combined
geographical interest?" What check had our government provided
against abuse of a "great local interest?" He found his answer in a
veto, nullification, or interposition, as the doctrine was variously
called.

Although Calhoun did not deny the abstract "right" of secession, he himself saw "peaceful, constitutional nullification" of the tariff law as the proper alternative. But Andrew Jackson did not see it that way, nor did the more rabid of the South Carolina hotheads, for whom disunion was the only answer. Meanwhile, Calhoun and Jackson had split irrevocably.

Although elected as Jackson's running mate, Calhoun had early incurred his chief's displeasure. The reasons were partly petty and social and stemmed from an incident at the inaugural ball, where the ranking lady of Washington society, Mrs. John C. Calhoun, had seemed not to "notice the presence of Mrs. Eaton." As Peggy O'Neale, Mrs. Eaton was rumored to have had a love affair with John Eaton, Jackson's Secretary of War, well before their recent marriage. The cabinet ladies followed Floride's example; Secretary of State Martin Van Buren stepped in and, by showering the Eatons with attention, ingratiated himself with Jackson. Calhoun was blamed for his wife's behavior.

Events now followed in rapid sequence. In January, 1830, with glowing eloquence, Daniel Webster made the cause of the expanding, industrializing North that of the Union itself, as he replied to South Carolina's spokesman for nullification, Senator Robert Young Hayne. Calhoun, as Vice-President, lean, taut, and intent, had sent notes of suggestion down to Hayne during his speech. In April, Calhoun was foremost among the nullification spokesmen arranging the annual Jefferson Day dinner at which both he and the President would offer volunteer toasts. Jackson flung down the challenge. "Our Federal Union," he said. "It must be preserved." And Calhoun, eyes blazing into Jackson's own, picked up the challenge and responded with his lifelong creed: "The Union," he said, "next to our liberties most dear." The battle lines of the future had been drawn.

The Jackson-Calhoun "break" became official and final a month later. Political skullduggery, shared in equal part by three who were no friends of Calhoun—Martin Van Buren, William H. Crawford, and Sam Houston—had brought a letter of tremendous import to Jackson's attention. It revealed that Calhoun, far from being Jackson's defender in Monroe's cabinet, had instead urged that he be reprimanded or investigated for his foray into Florida.

Although the whole cabinet with the exception of John Quincy Adams had taken the same stand, Jackson was infuriated. So far as he was concerned, Calhoun was finished, his presidential prospects at an end. Calhoun came to this realization slowly, and voiced personal support for Jackson well into the summer. Not until March, 1831,

did he admit that he had dissolved all ties with Jackson, "political
. . . or otherwise." Calhoun was now free to look to the South and
its defenses against the encroachments of a centralized, industrializing
North, committed to the "naked principle" of unchecked majority
rule. He was free to range himself behind South Carolina's cause, and
to admit openly in his public letter to Governor Hamilton his authorship and espousal of the Nullification Doctrine.

The country watched, fascinated, as Calhoun resigned the vice-
presidency, accepted election as Senator from South Carolina, and
marched upon Washington to do battle for his state. Charleston was
an armed camp and South Carolina, assembled in convention, had declared the tariff null and void in the state.

Andrew Jackson began to call for troops. Seven cutters and a war-
ship trained their guns upon the people of South Carolina. Jackson's
Proclamation of December Tenth, 1832, sounded like a bugle call. "Fellow citizens of my native state . . . ," he appealed, "to say that any
State may secede . . . is to say that the United States is not a nation.
. . . Disunion by armed forces is treason." More privately, he added
that the nullifiers could pass resolutions and agitate to their heart's content. "But if one drop of blood is shed there in defiance of the laws of
the United States," he promised, "I will hang the first man of them I
can get my hands on."

He was still talking about hanging when Calhoun arrived in Washington. All the way north, crowds had gathered to stare at the besieged
former Vice-President. When he entered the Senate chamber, friends
turned away; only after he had pledged his loyalty to the Constitution
of the United States did several come up and shake his hand.

Not since Benedict Arnold, one observer thought, had the fall of a
public man been so complete. Yet within a few weeks' time, feelings
softened towards him. No one who saw or heard Calhoun then, "logic
set on fire," as one described him, could doubt his passionate sincerity.
He was not a traitor but a fanatic and even those most prejudiced
came to understand his belief that he was "fulfilling the duty of a
true patriot."

Calhoun knew, of course, that he was supporting doctrines which
most of the people would consider "new and dangerous." His adversary now was Webster, who viewed nullification "as if one were to
take the plunge of Niagara and cry out that he would stop half-way
down." Logically, Calhoun and Webster fought each other to a standstill; constitutionally, Calhoun was able to demonstrate the validity
of nullification by Webster's own arguments of an earlier day. But
Webster spoke, not for what had been, but for what was to be, the

united and nationalized Union of the future, and public opinion massed on the New Englander's side.

Calhoun was fighting a two-pronged battle, not for nullification alone, but against Jackson's answer to nullification. This was the Force Bill or "bloody bill," as Calhoun called it, Jackson's demand for guns and troops to enforce the tariff in South Carolina. The bill was passed and Calhoun, foreshadowing the tragedy of a generation later, predicted that it would "be resisted at every hazard . . . even that of death. . . . It is madness to suppose that the Union can be preserved by force."

An impasse had been reached. But Henry Clay, spokesman for the Missouri Compromise of 1820, together with Calhoun, hammered out details of a new compromise settlement. Calhoun's next task was to speed to South Carolina and make sure that the Ordinance of Nullification was rescinded. He traveled night and day in the open mail coaches, the rain beating down upon him. When he arrived, the mood of the convention was ugly: the fire-eaters had no desire to accept peace from Henry Clay under the guns of Andrew Jackson. But most of the delegates had already decided they had no choice but to back down. They listened sullenly to Calhoun's pleadings as he begged South Carolina to "avert war in the South," not to betray the American hope of union. He had his way, but the convention saved face by "nullifying" the Force Bill. This action was completely meaningless, for Calhoun well knew that the "bloody bill' was on permanent record, that it recognized national authority as superior to state authority, and that under it a consolidated, centralized government had been effectually established. "The struggle," he wrote, "far from being over, has only just commenced." Wearily, he retreated to Fort Hill. He had looked into the abyss, and except for a few interludes at home, he was never to know rest or health or peace again.

Years later, writing in London upon the outbreak of the Civil War, William Ellery Channing was to define its origins as a conspiracy of the slave states to ruin because they could not rule and extend slavery, the home of this conspiracy being South Carolina and the "Grand Master of the conspirators being the late John C. Calhoun." Channing quoted Jackson, who had declared the tariff to be merely the pretext of the Nullifiers, their real design being "Disunion and a Southern Confederacy. . . . The next pretext will be the Negro or Slavery question." And even Calhoun admitted privately that this was the real issue.

Yet it is certain that Calhoun advanced nullification as a device to forestall South Carolina's secession and to preserve the Union. He believed in the preservation of a Union of coequal states, but a union coexistent with slavery, and this belief was the tragic contradiction that marred his thinking. Slavery, as Jackson had seen, was the unbidden guest at the nullification feast. Yet Calhoun had mentioned it only in passing. When resisting the idea that the South could also industrialize and compete with the North, he warned that those who now warred upon Southern agriculture "would do it upon our labor."

The defense of slavery within the Union as essential to the Southern way of life was to be Calhoun's tortured concern for the rest of his life. The only alternatives he saw were enforced emancipation or secession or both. There were still moments, interludes, when his latent nationalism flared: when as Secretary of State he brought Texas into the Union (although even here he invoked the slavery question); during his great speeches on the Oregon annexation, when he helped avert war with England and evoked a vision of one world; in his call for a "balanced industry," a balanced Union at the Memphis Convention where he urged internal improvements upon our great rivers, our "inland seas."

During his last years, when his intellect was at its most incandescent, he wrote the two books upon which his reputation as a political philosopher rests: *A Disquisition on Government* and *A Discourse on the Constitution of the United States*. In these books he discussed in full his revolutionary doctrine of the concurrent majority, of which nullification was but one aspect—his concept of a government, not "of a part over a part," but of "a part made identical with the whole," each division or "interest" armed with either a voice in making the laws, "or a veto on their execution." He recognized that "only a few great and prominent interests could be represented," but even Richard Hofstadter acknowledges that "Calhoun's analysis of American political tensions certainly ranks among the most impressive intellectual achievements of American statesmen." [2] Arthur Schlesinger, Jr., on the other hand, while conceding that Calhoun's theory was devised to protect a special group, denies that it was any mere lawyer's brief "to advance the pretensions of slavery, but a brilliant and penetrating study of modern society, whose insights remain vital for any minority." [3]

As for slavery, the more Calhoun saw its doom, the more passionately he argued for its preservation. He knew that the North was rapidly

[2] Richard Hofstadter, *The American Political Tradition* (New York, 1948), pp. 87–88.

[3] Arthur Schlesinger, Jr., *The Age of Jackson* (Boston and New York, 1945), p. 405.

outnumbering the South, that simple majority rule was ever more the law of the land. He knew that, whipped on by the abolitionist minority, more and more people were coming to see slavery as a sin and any compromise with slave-holders as treason. The South was at bay, her way of life and her "peculiar institution" doomed.

Yet, for all the power and clarity of his thinking, Calhoun saw no way out of the dilemma. Even had he seriously considered abolition as a possibility—an act which would have ended his public life and fame—there seemed to be no feasible answers. Colonization was impractical; the freedmen did not want to go back to Africa. The life of a freed black could be miserable, as Calhoun discovered for himself when he freed a shoemaker who later came back from the North and begged to be reinslaved.[4] Even some of the new "free" states denied settlement to freed men. The North had no plans beyond abolition; the South had even less, because the Southerners saw no way out of what, even more than an economic question, was a social one. How, other than by slavery, were the relations between the races to be regulated?

Hence, as Calhoun said, he was determined to meet the enemy on the frontier, convinced that attempted forcible destruction of slavery would mean secession and the dissolution of the Union. He came even to hail slavery as "a good, a positive good," the only possible solution to an impossible dilemma.

The battle broke out before the Jackson administration ended. Incendiary abolitionist pamphlets were arousing agitation in the South; Jackson had called for a federal law prohibiting their distribution. Calhoun countered this, arguing that Congress had no more power to interfere with the mails than it had to abolish slavery. Instead, Calhoun suggested that federal post-office agents be required to aid local postal officials in preventing the circulation of abolitionist material.

Abolitionist petitions posed a parallel problem. For years, despite the unyielding opposition of John Quincy Adams in the House, the so-called "Gag Rule" automatically tabled without debate all petitions concerning the abolition of slavery. Calhoun and his followers had secured this "gag," but with every battle they won they came closer to losing the war.

The great struggle came over the fate of the territories. Like other

[4] The incident of the returned slave was observed by the Calhoun family governess, Mary Bates. See Mary Bates, *The Private Life of John C. Calhoun* (Charleston, 1852), p. 21.

good men, including Daniel Webster, Calhoun opposed the Mexican war,[5] one of the most controversial struggles we have ever engaged in. Calhoun was opposed to the conflict because of its naked aggressiveness, because of the cost in blood and treasure, and because the manner of its declaration gave the President, apart from Congress, the power to make war. "Mexico," Calhoun said, "is to us the forbidden fruit." Most of all, he feared the controversy that would ensue over territories which might be won from Mexico, which the North would never see slave and the South would never see free.

David Wilmot's "Proviso" that slavery be barred from all lands acquired by the Mexican War, marked the culmination of Calhoun's greatest fears. So he counterattacked, contending that the territories belonged to all the states, and that any citizen had a right to migrate anywhere with his "property," yes, even to Oregon. Yet to keep the peace, he agreed to President Polk's completely logical and reasonable suggestion that the Missouri Compromise line be extended to the Pacific. Most Northerners repudiated this so-called solution (although a few years later, in the wake of "popular sovereignty," they would be calling the Missouri Compromise sacred, and a part of the Constitution). The issue, they said, was one of principle. To the North, slavery was a sin; to the South, a right, and between these two extremes there could be no compromise.

Calhoun had long realized that Southern nationalism was a viable force and that to organize it within the Union was the only way to keep it from destroying the Union. Hence, his "Southern Address," in which he warned that if the North had the power to control the territories, it could also free the slaves and reduce the Southern whites to poverty and political subjugation. Only unity, political and sectional, against the aggressions of the North, only a kind of dominion status for the South, could save her. During the "deepening agony" of what were now his last days, he grasped at any straw rather than advise the South to submit to the ultimate remedy, secession. He simply could not bear to see the end of the Union he had loved and served for so long. Even in illness, his mind was grappling feverishly with the problem; his doctor said he was literally "thinking himself into the grave."

Yet he saw no way out in the compromise hammered together by Clay and Webster in the winter of 1850. The wounds had gone too

[5] Ironically, Calhoun's role in the annexation of Texas had helped precipitate the conflict.

deep. Too weak to speak, he sat by, ghostlike, wrapped in his cloak, gesturing passionately, his eyes glowing "with meteor-like brilliance," as his last tragic warning was read for him by Senator James Mason of Virginia.

The equilibrium, he said, that had once existed between North and South had been shattered. The national government had become centralized, crushing out the rights of the states; the cords of the Union, of plighted faith and fellowship, the spiritual ties between the churches—all were broken. Only a union of force remained.

Could the Union be saved? Only if the North *willed* it, ceased "agitation of the slavery question," conceded the South equal rights in the territories, and consented to a constitutional amendment, artificially restoring that broken equilibrium between the sections. He had no compromise to offer, no ground to stand on but the Constitution. If the North would not give way, or let the states "part in peace," the South would not shrink from what it had to do.

In his insistence upon a constitutional, rather than a congressional, settlement, Calhoun was, of course, aware that any mere compromise by Congress could be readily undone by a subsequent Congress. What he would not face was that ultimately even the Constitution rests upon the will of the people to uphold it.

Calhoun had done. He appeared briefly three more times in the Senate, once during Webster's great speech on the seventh of March, when again the South Carolinian offered conciliation, calling for the extension of the Missouri Compromise line to the Pacific. As for the Union, Calhoun warned: "Great moral causes will break it if they go on." At last, he was fully aware of the North's determination.

"The South—the poor South! God knows what will become of her!" had been his cry the year before, but now his thoughts were obsessed by the coming "dissolution of the Union." He foresaw this dissolution within ten years' time. "The probability is that it will explode in a presidential election."

In the future, he saw civil war, the conquest of the South, the agonies of Reconstruction, the defeat of all that he had fought for and held dear. His life, one historian has written, was a perfect tragedy. To the end, he kept searching, hoping for a way out. "I cannot help from thinking about the country," he said on his deathbed. He was still seeking to reconcile irreconcilables, to save the Union and the South within the Union.

On Sunday, March 31, 1850, his luminous eyes closed forever. On his tomb in St. Philip's churchyard in Charleston was placed the one word, CALHOUN. Years later, a bitter Yankee soldier pronounced a fitting epitaph: "The whole South," he said, "is the grave of Calhoun."

The enormous project of publishing *The Papers of John C. Calhoun*, estimated to run about fifteen volumes, has brought thousands of hitherto unknown Calhoun papers into the offices of the South Caroliniana Library in Columbia. According to the project editor, Dr. W. Edwin Hemphill, Calhoun remains consistent; the generally accepted picture of him is basically the same, "although he is revealed as a far better Secretary of War than we had ever known."

Among the most interesting accessions are a series of letters Calhoun wrote to Samuel D. Ingham, Pennsylvania congressman and Jackson's first Secretary of the Treasury. Calhoun and Ingham were warm personal friends; with him, Calhoun wrote, he was under no restraint in expressing his feelings. The excerpts quoted below include a still comparatively youthful Calhoun's overoptimistic and idealized picture of himself as a presidential candidate in 1822; a bitter personal attack on Jackson, Van Buren, and Eaton during the Peggy O'Neale controversy, in which Calhoun revealed himself as a bad political prophet where Jackson was concerned, and a good one regarding Van Buren. The third letter displays his feelings in the midst of the whirling storm center of the new doctrine of Nullification.[6]

From the War Department, Calhoun wrote on April 5, 1822, that it would be "*mere* affectation" for him not to admit that he was personally gratified at the pleasure his Presidential candidacy had excited, "but I would be wholly unworthy of the preference, which my friends have given me for the highest trust of the nation, if the preponderance of pleasure were on that account. I know I am, without any self-deception, much more attached to *the cause* than to my personal advancement. I would much rather go down in pursuing, that system of policy to which I am attached, than to rise by persuing [*sic*] any other. The happiness and greatness of our country have, from early youth, been my first object. These are best advanced, by what I consider the highest Republican principle, a fixed confidence in the virtue and intelligence of the people. With such a confidence, a conviction must follow, that the best way to rise is to do right, to pursue with prudence the lasting *interest* of the country. This I have endeavoured to do, and the favour, with which as a publick man, I

am regarded by the American People, is, on no account more grati-
fying to me, than that it affords additional evidence, that to serve them
honestly is the way to win their favour. . . ."

From Fort Hill, on May 4, 1831, he wrote: "What a game of cunning & duplicity your two late associates in the administration, who
first resigned [Martin Van Buren and John H. Eaton], had attempted
to play on the country, and, what is still worse, that the President
[Andrew Jackson] himself is ready to take a subordinate part in so
disgraceful a transaction.

"Take Mr. Van Beuren's [sic] statement and according to his own
showing, it will be impossible for him to escape disgrace. His letter
rests, when well considered, on the foll[ow]ing grounds; that he is
already, six years before the time, a candidate to succeed Genl.
Jackson, that he has been anxious to keep the fact out of view; but
has not been able to do so, that he is in consequence of its disclosure,
and the distracting effect it has on the administration, reduced to the
alternative to leave the administration, or to abandon his prospects
of succeeding Genl. Jackson, that, tho[ugh] the period is highly critical
and dangerous, he prefers abandoning his friend, the President, his
party and the country, to relinquishing the prospect of succession.
. . . The President has taken a part in the question of his successor, . . . and the measures of his administration, are to be made
subservient to that object; and thus his friend Van Beuren [sic] is to
have the whole influence of the Government in his favour, without
the odium or responsibility. . . .

"I have long believed, that Genl. Jackson is unworthy of his station,
and that to continue him six years longer would utterly ruin his
reputation, and *destroy* the party. . . . This last occurrence has convinced me that something must be done. . . . The two leading ap-
pointments in the new administration . . . may be fairly considered
as . . . most disgracefully purchased, by subserviency to Mrs. Eaton;
and but too clearly show, what may be expected under the new order
of things. The declaration of Mr. Van Beuren [sic] to Mrs. McLean,
that if she would call on Mrs. Eaton it would be of service to the
future prospect of her husband, is now interpreted . . . I consider
Genl. Jackson in the South not only weak, but in fact odious, with
but little exception, perhaps in Georgia, where the Indian question,
has strengthened him. In fact, the very pretex[t] for his run[n]ing a
second time has failed. It could have no plausible motive . . . but
. . . to give a triumph to the principles on which he was supported. . . . He has abandon[ed] the principle, on which he was self-
elevated. We opposed the late administration, expressly on the ground,

not only, that Mr. Adams was elected against the publick will, but that his administration was pledged to the elevation of Mr. Clay, as his successor; the evidence of which, as strong as it was, is not stronger, than that Genl. Jackson is pledged to aid Mr. V[an Bure]n to the chair of state. These are my views, and, in my opinion, this is our time as patriots and Republicans to save the country from embarrassment & the party from ruin. . . ."

Four months later, Calhoun's thoughts were on a different topic, nullification. Writing on September 8, he acknowledged Ingham's "favourable opinion," which coming from a man of his judgment and integrity was "above all price. . . . I could not expect to command the assent of the inattentive, the interested, or the prejudiced. The most, I could hope was the approbation of the intelligent & disinterested. I feel the most certain conviction, that on no other principle can our federal system be maintained; and that, on the opposite, it cannot last a single generation. Had my love of Union & the constitution been less, or ambition greater, I certainly would not have ventured the step I have. I put all to hazard for my country, and shall be satisfied, if she should be benefitted, tho[ugh] it should consign me to the shades of retirement for life. It appears to me, the remedy will be more safe standing on the reserved rights of the State, without any express constitutional provision. . . .

"I do hope all the old and experienced Democrats of '98 will see, when they come to reflect, that I have originated no new doctrine, but have simply revised & illustrated those of the purest period of the party. It is really melancholy to reflect, that the principles which elevated Jefferson & were supported by McKean, should now be considered treason. . . .

"I firmly believe with you, that Jackson is both insincere and corrupt. He cannot be supported without destroying the Republican party. I, for one, cannot give him my support . . . it would be better that Clay should be forced on us, than that we should participate in the continuance of Jackson in power. In the former case, the Republican party may again be rallied; and lead [sic] to victory; but, in the latter, it would perish in its own corruption. I speak, I am sure, on this point, the sentiment of this State."

Calhoun always wrote on an intimate basis to his Yale classmate Micah Sterling, whose son, John Calhoun, was his godson. He did not hesitate to use his influence to get his namesake into West Point: "I think the prospect of Mr. [Martin] Van Beuren['s] [sic] election good. The prospect is, that he will take all of the slaveholding States except Kentucky. I am glad to learn that his prospect improves in N[ew] York.

"It would be well to make the application for . . . my name sake some time before hand. If you will transmit his application to me, when the proper time arrives for the application, say six months or a year before his admission, it will afford me much pleasure to attend to it.

"My health is good, and I feel but little as yet the [effects] of age, but I know that I have arrived at the period, when old may be well prefaced to my name. I look with perfect composure on the advance of time, knowing that it is in the order of Providence and that it is our highest duty to acquiesce in his decrees. My confidence in his wisdom & goodness is without limits, and has been the support, which has sustained me through all the vicissitudes of life. . . . I shall be happy to see John [Calhoun Sterling] when he visits the South & hope he may make his arrangement to spend some time with me."

Chronology of the Life of John C. Calhoun

1782	(March 18) Born at Abbeville District, South Carolina, son of Patrick and Martha (Caldwell) Calhoun.
1800–02	At school at Moses Waddell's "log college."
1802	Enters Yale as a Junior.
1804	(September 12) Graduates from Yale.
1805–06	At Tapping Reeves's law school, Litchfield, Connecticut.
1807	Begins the practice of law in Abbeville, South Carolina. (October) Elected to the South Carolina General Assembly where he serves two years.
1810	(October) Elected to the first of three terms in the United States House of Representatives, Twelfth Congress.
1811	(January 8) Marries his cousin, Floride Bonneau Calhoun.
1811	(November 4) Starts his congressional career. (December 12) First speech on war resolutions.
1812	(June 3) Introduces bill for war against Great Britain.
1812–17	As Representative, Calhoun supports incorporation of the Second National Bank, a protective tariff, and governmental expenditures for internal improvements.
1817	(October 8) Becomes Secretary of War in the administration of President James Monroe.
1819	(January 14) Reports on development of roads and canals.
1821	Announces his candidacy for the Presidency of the United States.
1824	(December 3) Second report on the development of roads and canals. Elected Vice-President of the United States, under John Q. Adams.
1825	Makes Fort Hill plantation, Pendleton, South Carolina, his permanent residence. (March 4) Sworn in as Vice-President.
1827	Defeats the Woolens Bill for raising the tariff by breaking a tie vote in the Senate.
1828	Anonymously writes "The South Carolina Exposition and Protest," which is adopted, with modifications, in December by the South Carolina Legislature.

	(November) Elected Vice-President of the United States, under Andrew Jackson.
1831	William Lloyd Garrison issues *The Liberator*.
	The Nat Turner rebellion breaks out in Virginia.
1831–32	Break with President Andrew Jackson.
1831	(July 26) Letter to the people of South Carolina.
1832	(July 16) Resigns from the Vice-Presidency.
	(August 28) Letter to Governor Hamilton.
	(December 12) Elected to the United States Senate by the South Carolina Legislature.
1833	(February) Defends nullification and debates with Webster in the United States Senate. Joins with Henry Clay in support of a compromise tariff bill.
1834	Battles Andrew Jackson's national bank policies.
1836	(March 9) Speech on Abolition Petitions.
1837	Defends slavery as a "positive good." Supports the Van Buren independent treasury program.
1838	(March 10) Reply to Henry Clay.
1841	Leads the battle against the Whig program in Congress and seeks the Democratic presidential nomination.
1843	Retires from the Senate to seek the Presidency and starts work on his two books, *A Disquisition on Government* and *A Discourse on the Constitution of the United States*.
1844	(January 20th) Withdraws from consideration as a presidential candidate.
	(March 6th) Becomes Secretary of State under President John Tyler. Negotiates Texas annexation treaty which fails in the Senate. Draws up joint resolution for annexation which passes the two houses of Congress.
1845	(November 26) Reelected to the United States Senate. Presides over Memphis Railroad Convention.
1846	(March 16) Speech on the Oregon question. Opposes going to war with Mexico.
1847	(February 9) Speech on the Three Million Bill.
	(February 19) Speech on the resolutions regarding the Wilmot Proviso. Calls for Southern unity.
	(March 9) Speech to the citizens of Charleston.
1848	(January 4) Speech on his resolutions on the war with Mexico.
	(June 27) Speech demanding that Oregon Territory be open to slavery.
1849	Strives to rally the Southern congressmen to a united

stand and almost completes his two books,
the *Disquisition* and *Discourse*.

1850   (March 4) Last speech read to the Senate by Senator James
Mason of Virginia.
(March 13) Last remarks in the Senate.
(March 31) Dies in Washington.

1957   Named one of the five great Senators of all time by
vote of the United States Senate.

PART ONE

JOHN C. CALHOUN LOOKS AT THE WORLD

In this section are presented extracts from some of Calhoun's more important speeches and letters. The speeches were delivered in the House of Representatives (1811–1817) and in the United States Senate (1833–1850). The texts are as printed in the first published edition of Calhoun's Works, *edited by Richard Crallé, 6 volumes (New York, 1854–1857).*

1
War and Peace

I will lay it down as an universal criterion, that a war is offensive or defensive, not by the mode of carrying it on . . . but by the motive and cause that lead to it.

—CALHOUN

There is often, in the affairs of government, more efficiency and wisdom in non-action than in action.

—CALHOUN

Mexico is to us the forbidden fruit; the penalty of eating it would be to subject our institutions to political death.

—CALHOUN

ON THE GOALS OF THE WAR [1]

Although foremost among those who whipped the young nation into the vastly unpopular War of 1812, Calhoun was con-

[1] From speech "On the Loan Bill" (February 25, 1814), Crallé, ed., *Works,* II, 88–91, 98.

vinced that war should never be resorted to unless it was clearly necessary. He believed that the conflict with England was a struggle for national independence against intolerable wrongs.

From the flood the tide dates its ebb; from the meridian, the sun commences his decline. There is more of sound philosophy than fiction in the fickleness which poets attribute to fortune. Prosperity has its weakness—adversity its strength. In many respects our enemy has lost by those very changes which seem to be so much in his favor. He can now no more claim to be struggling for existence; no more, to be fighting the battles of the world, in defence of the liberties of mankind. The magic cry of *French influence,* is lost. . . . The great monopolist of the ocean will, I trust, be the next object of fear and resistance. . . . Ever since the discovery of the passage round the Cape of Good Hope, and of this continent, on which we enjoy the proud pre-eminence of being the first great civilized power, a great change has been gradually working in Europe. For two centuries, the character of that part of the world has been eminently trading and commercial. . . . It is impossible they can behold with indifference the monopoly of Great Britain. They will not quietly suffer the common highway of nations, intended by a kind Providence for the common intercourse and benefit of all, to be converted into her exclusive domain. No; the ocean cannot become property. Like light and air, it is insusceptible of the idea of property. Heaven has given it to man equally, freely, bountifully; and all empires attempted to be raised on it, must partake of the fickleness of its waves. A policy so injurious to the common interests of mankind, must, sooner or later, unite the world against her. . . . Liberated not from fear, they will soon have leisure to attend to their interests. . . . But if, unfortunately, we should be left alone to maintain the contest; and if, in consequence (which may God forbid), necessity should compel us to yield for the present, yet our generous efforts will not have been in vain. A mode of thinking, and a tone of sentiment have been excited, which must stimulate to future and more successful struggles. What we may not be able to effect with eight millions of people, will be done with twenty. The great cause will not be yielded. No; never! never! We cannot renounce our rights to the ocean which Providence has spread before our doors; nor will we ever hold that, which is the immediate gift of Heaven, under the license of any nation. We have already had success worthy of our cause. The future is audibly pronounced by

he splendid victories over the Gueriere, Java, and Macedonian. . . .
The charm of British naval invincibility is broken.

In this, the only just view of our contest, how pitiful appear the
objections of our opponents! Some *pecuniary difficulties* in Massachu-
etts, and in other places! And must we, for them, renounce our lasting
prosperity and greatness? Have we no fortitude?—no self-command?
Must we, like children, yield to the impulse of present pleasure, however fatal? If the maritime parts of Massachusetts suffer, let them
remember, that if the war should be successful—if our future commerce and navigation should be secured, they will partake most largely
in the advantages, common and great, indeed, to all, but peculiarly
so to them.

* * *

How far the minority in a state of war, may justly oppose the
measures of Government, is a question of the greatest delicacy. On
he one side, an honest man, if he believe the war to be unjust or
unwise, will not disavow his opinion. But, on the other hand, an upright citizen will do no act, whatever he may think of the war, to put
his country in the power of the enemy. It is this double aspect of the
subject which indicates the course that reason approves. Among ourselves, at home, we may contend; but whatever may be requisite to
give the reputation and arms of the republic a superiority over its
enemy, it is the duty of all, the minority no less than the majority,
to support. Like the system of our State and General governments,—
within, they are many,—to the world but one,—so it ought to be
with parties:—among ourselves, we may divide,—but in relation to
other nations, there ought to be only the American people. In some
cases it may possibly be doubtful, even to the most conscientious,
how to act. This is one of the misfortunes of differing from the rest
of the community on the subject of war.

ON THE CONSTITUTION'S TREATY-MAKING POWER

*Here Calhoun shows for the first time the love for constitu-
tional theory and analysis which is characteristic of his later
years. He also reveals that in his early years in Congress he was
no apologist for slavery.*

The grant of the power to make treaties is couched in the most
general terms. The words of the constitution are, that the President

shall have power, by and with the advice and consent of the Senate to make treaties, provided two-thirds of the Senators present concur In a subsequent part of the constitution, treaties are declared to be the supreme law of the land. Whatever limits are imposed by these general terms ought to be the result of a sound construction of the instrument. There are, apparently, but two restrictions on its exercise the one derived from the nature of our government, and the othe from that of the power itself. Most certainly all grants of power unde the constitution must be construed by that instrument; for, having their existence from it, they must of necessity assume that form which the constitution has imposed. This is acknowledged to be true of the legislative power, and it is doubtless equally so of the power to make treaties. The limits of the former are exactly marked; it was necessary to prevent collision with similar co-existing State powers. This countr is divided into many distinct sovereignties. Exact enumeration o this head is necessary, to prevent the most dangerous consequences The enumeration of legislative powers in the constitution has re lation, then, not to the treaty-making power, but to the powers o the States. In our relation to the rest of the world the case is reversed Here the States disappear. Divided within, we present the exterior o undivided sovereignty. The wisdom of the constitution, in this, ap pears conspicuous. Where enumeration was needed, there we find th powers enumerated and exactly defined; where not, we do not fine what would be only vain and pernicious. Whatever, then, concern our foreign relations; whatever requires the consent of another nation belongs to the treaty-making power, and can only be regulated by it and it is competent to regulate all such subjects, provided (and her are its true limits) such regulations are not inconsistent with the constitution. If so, they are void. No treaty can alter the fabric o our government, nor can it do that which the constitution has ex pressly forbidden to be done; nor can it do that differently which i directed to be done in a given mode,—all other modes being pro hibited. For instance, the constitution says, no money "shall be drawn out of the treasury but by an appropriation made by law." Of cours no subsidy can be granted without an act of law; and a treaty of al liance could not involve the country in war without the consent o this House. With this limitation, it is easy to explain the case put b my colleague, who said, that according to one limitation, a treat might have prohibited the introduction of a certain description o persons before the year 1808, notwithstanding the clause in the consti tution to the contrary. I will speak plainly on this point:—it was the intention of the constitution that the slave trade should be tolerated ill the time mentioned. It covers me with confusion to name it here; feel ashamed of such a tolerance, and take a large part of the disgrace, as I represent a part of the Union by whose influence it might e supposed to have been introduced. Though Congress alone is prohibited, by the words of the clause, from suppressing that odious traffic, yet my colleague will admit that it was intended to be a general prohibition on the Government of the Union.[2]

I know of no situation so responsible, if properly considered, as ours. We are charged by Providence, not only with the happiness of this great and rising people, but, in a considerable degree, with that of the human race. We have a government of a new order, perfectly distinct from all others which have preceded it—a government founded on the rights of man; resting, not on authority, not on prejudice, not on superstition, but reason. If it shall succeed, as fondly hoped by its founders, it will be the commencement of a new era in human affairs. All civilized governments must, in the course of time, conform to its principles. Thus circumstanced, can you hesitate what course to choose? The road that wisdom indicates, leads, it is true, up the steep, but leads also to security and lasting glory. No nation that wants the fortitude to tread it, ought ever to aspire to greatness.[3]

ON THE OREGON BILL

Calhoun's innate patriotism and latent nationalism were never more evident than in his stand on the controversial Oregon question. He wanted "all of the territory, as much as we could get without war with England," but was convinced that time— and destiny—would gain most of the territory for us.

My object is to preserve, and not to lose the territory.

* * *

All we want, to effect our object in this case, is "a wise and masterly inactivity." Our population is rolling towards the shores of the Pacific with an impetus greater than what we realize. It is one of those for-

[2] From speech "On the Bill to Regulate the Commerce Between the United States and Great Britain" (January 9, 1816), Crallé, ed., *Works*, II, 132–33.

[3] From speech "On the Motion to Repeal the Direct Tax" (January 31, 1816), Crallé, ed., *Works*, II, 152.

ward movements which leaves anticipation behind. In the period o thirty-two years which have elapsed since I took my seat in the othe House, the Indian frontier has receded a thousand miles to th West. At that time our population was much less than half what i is now. It was then increasing at the rate of about a quarter of million annually; it is now not less than six hundred thousand,— and still increasing at the rate of something more than three pe cent, compound annually. At that rate, it will soon reach the yearl increase of a million.[4]

At no period has it ever been so desirable to preserve the genera peace which now blesses the world. Never in its history has a perio occurred so remarkable as that which has elapsed since the terminatio of the great war in Europe, with the battle of Waterloo, for the grea advances made in all these particulars. Chemical and mechanica discoveries and inventions have multiplied beyond all former example —adding, with their advance, to the comforts of life in a degree fa greater and more universal than all that was ever known before Civilization has, during the same period, spread its influence far an wide, and the general progress in knowledge, and its diffusion throug all ranks of society, has outstripped all that has ever gone before it The two great agents of the physical world have become subject to th will of man, and have been made subservient to his wants and enjoy ments; I allude to steam and electricity, under whatever name th latter may be called. The former has overcome distance both on lanc and water, to an extent which former generations had not the leas conception was possible. It has, in effect, reduced the Atlantic to hal its former width, while, at the same time, it has added three-fold to the rapidity of intercourse by land. Within the same period, electricity the greatest and most diffuse of all known physical agents, has bee made the instrument for the transmission of thought, I will not sa with the rapidity of lightning, but by lightning itself. Magic wire are stretching themselves in all directions over the earth, and whe their mystic meshes shall have been united and perfected, our glob itself will become endowed with sensitiveness,—so that whateve touches on any one point, will be instantly felt on every other. Al these improvements—all this increasing civilization—all the progres now making, would be in a great measure arrested by a war betwee us and Great Britain.

* * *

[4] From speech "On the Oregon Bill" (January 24, 1843), Crallé, ed., *Works,* IV 244–45.

I am finally opposed to war, because peace—peace is preeminently our policy. . . . Our great mission, as a people, is to occupy this vast domain; to replenish it with an intelligent, virtuous, and industrious population; to convert the forests into cultivated fields; to drain the swamps and morasses, and cover them with rich harvests; to build up cities, towns, and villages in every direction, and to unite the whole by the most rapid intercourse between all the parts. War would but impede the fulfillment of this high mission, by absorbing the means and diverting the energies which would be devoted to the purpose.[5]

ON THE MEXICAN WAR [6]

Calhoun was strongly opposed to the war with Mexico. He felt that it established a precedent by which the President, not Congress, could declare war; he saw it as a ruthless, aggressive war of conquest against a weak and helpless people; and he knew that the territory to be won would be laid open for conflict between the North, which would never permit it to be slave, and the South, which would never permit it to be free. Midway in the war, he contended that we had won our objectives and should halt and save lives by not marching on to Vera Cruz. He appealed to the Senators as Christians to stop the fighting, for we could hold all that we had won. In taking this stand, he sided with the North, which was generally opposed to the war, and sacrificed much of his popularity in the South—and with it, his last prospects for the Presidency.

How is peace to be obtained? It can only be by treaty; War may be made by one nation, but peace can only be made by two. The object then is to obtain a treaty; but what treaty? one that will suit Mexico? That can be obtained at any time. No, the treaty which is wanted is one that will suit us; but how can this be effected, but by compelling Mexico, by force of our arms, *and at our dictation,* to agree to such terms as we may dictate; and what could these terms be, but to secure all the objects for which the war was declared; that is, as has been

[5] From speech "On the Resolutions Giving Notice to Great Britain" (March 16, 1846), Crallé, ed., *Works*, IV, 283–84, 285.
[6] From speech "On the 'Three Million Bill'" (February 9, 1847), Crallé ed., *Works*, IV, 316–17, 323.

shown, to establish the Rio del Norte as our western boundary, and
to obtain ample territory as the only means of our indemnity?

The intention, then, is to compel Mexico to acknowledge that to be
ours which we now hold, and can, as I have already shown, easily hold,
without her consent. This is all—more or less cannot be made of it.
But how is Mexico to be compelled to sign such a treaty? We are
informed that, for that purpose, the intention, in the first place, is to
take Vera Cruz, and the Castle of San Juan de Ulloa, and then to
march to the city of Mexico, and there to dictate the treaty. Now,
with this object in view, I ask the Senate, Is it worth while to pursue a
vigorous war to compel Mexico to acknowledge that to be ours, which
we hold, and can easily hold, against her consent? Is it worthwhile,
even if we were perfectly certain of complete success by taking Vera
Cruz and marching to Mexico, and there dictating a treaty at the end
of this campaign? What would be the sacrifice, in effecting this, of men
and money? The army authorized to be raised is about 70,000 men,
and the expense of the campaign may be put at $30,000,000. It will
probably exceed it by several millions, but I desire to be moderate.
Suppose the active force in the field be 50,000 men, what then will be
your sacrifice under this supposition? The loss of $30,000,000. And
what the sacrifice of life will be, may be judged by looking at the
past. One-third must be put down as certain to perish, not by the
sword only, but by disease. Sixteen thousand lives then must be
sacrificed. Now, I put it home to you, Senators.—Is it worthwhile to
make this immense sacrifice of money and men for the mere purpose
of obtaining the consent of Mexico to hold what we can so easily
hold in despite of her? I put a graver question. I appeal to the conscience of every Senator who hears me, can you, as a Christian, justify
giving a vote that would lead to such results?

*   *   *

How shall the territory be disposed of if any should be acquired?
Shall it be for the benefit of one part of the Union to the exclusion
of the other? We are told,—and I fear that appearances justify it,—
that all parties in the non-slaveholding States are united in the
determination that they shall have the exclusive benefit and monopoly
—that such provisions shall be made by treaty or law, as to exclude
all who hold slaves in the South from emigrating with their property
into the acquired country. If the non-slaveholding States having no
other interest but an aversion to our domestic institutions (for such is
slavery as it exists in the South),—if, I repeat, they can come to the

conclusion, to exclude the South from all benefit in the acquired territory, with no other interest but that, I turn to their representatives on this floor and ask them, what they suppose must be the feeling of the slaveholding States, to whom this question is one of safety and not of mere policy, to be deprived of their rights, and their perfect equality secured by the constitution, and to be assailed in their most vulnerable point? Be assured, if there be stern determination on one side to exclude us, there will be determination still sterner on ours, not to be excluded.

2
The Broadening Union

The Union, next to our liberties most dear.

—CALHOUN

From the very beginning of his career Calhoun was aware of the threat of eventual disunion. He saw our diversity and great distances as dangers and supported a program of internal improvements that would weld the union into a whole.

ON THE DANGER OF DISUNION [1]

Such is the happy mould of our Government—so wisely are the State and General powers arranged—that much of our political happiness derives its origin from the extent of our republic. It has exempted us from most of the causes which distracted the small republics of antiquity. Let it not, however, be forgotten; let it be for ever kept in mind that it exposes us to the greatest of all calamities—next to the loss of liberty—and even to that in its consequence —disunion. We are great, and rapidly—I was about to say fearfully— growing. This is our pride and our danger; our weakness and our strength. Little does he deserve to be intrusted with the liberties of this people, who does not raise his mind to these truths. We are under the most imperious obligation to counteract every tendency to disunion. The strongest of all cements is, undoubtedly, the wisdom, justice, and above all, the moderation of this House; yet the great subject on which we are now deliberating, in this respect deserves the most serious consideration. ⌊Whatever impedes the intercourse of the extremes with this, the centre of the republic, weakens the union⌋ The more enlarged the sphere of commercial circulation—the more extended that of intercourse—the more strongly are we bound together

[1] From speech "On the Bill to Set Aside the Bank Bill Dividends" (February 4, 1817), Crallé, ed., *Works*, II, 190–91.

—the more inseparable are our destinies. Those who understand the human heart best know how powerfully distance tends to break the sympathies of our nature. Nothing—not even dissimilarity of language —tends more to estrange man from man. Let us, then, bind the republic together with a perfect system of roads and canals. Let us conquer space. It is thus the most distant parts of the republic will be brought within a few days' travel of the centre; it is thus that a citizen of the West will read the news of Boston still moist from the press. The mail and the press are the nerves of the body politic. By them, the slightest impression made on the most remote parts, is communicated to the whole system; and the more perfect the means of transportation, the more rapid and true the vibration. To aid us in this great work—to maintain the integrity of this republic, we inhabit a country presenting the most admirable advantages. Belted around, as it is, by lakes and oceans—intersected in every direction by bays and rivers, the hand of industry and art is tempted to improvement. So situated, blessed with a form of government at once combining liberty and strength, we may reasonably raise our eyes to a most splendid future, if we only act in a manner worthy of our advantages. If, however, neglecting them, we permit a low, sordid, selfish and sectional spirit to take possession of this House, this happy scene will vanish. We will divide;—and in its consequences will follow, misery and despotism.

To legislate for our country, requires not only the most enlarged views, but a species of self-devotion not exacted in any other. In a country so extensive, and so various in its interests, what is necessary for the common good may apparently be opposed to the interest of particular sections. It must be submitted to as the condition of our greatness. But were we a small republic; were we confined to the ten miles square, the selfish instincts of our nature might, in most cases, be relied on in the management of public affairs.

3
Nullification

A deep constitutional question lies at the bottom of the controversy. The real question at issue is: Has the Government a right to impose burdens on the capital and industry of one portion of the country, not with a view to revenue, but to benefit another?

—CALHOUN

Power can only be opposed by power . . . and on this theory stands our beautiful federal system.

—CALHOUN

Nullification, Calhoun once said, was the word that he would like printed upon his tombstone. The doctrine was not original with him. It derived from Thomas Jefferson's and James Madison's Kentucky and Virginia Resolutions, from the Hartford Convention, from Daniel Webster's youthful warning that state governments could "interpose between their citizens and arbitrary power," and from the writings of Robert Turnbull. But Calhoun fused the parts, not only into an immediate political program, but into an entire philosophy of government. Yet his authorship of the first public expression of the doctrine, the "South Carolina Exposition and Protest," was kept secret—though suspected—as long as he cherished presidential ambitions. Nullification as a doctrine was generally looked upon as "new and dangerous," and Jackson eventually came to regard Calhoun as the instigator of the mischief in South Carolina. In fact, nullification was merely the reflection of deep-seated unrest, and in Calhoun's opinion a way out short of secession.

In the "South Carolina Exposition and Protest," Calhoun outlined the economics of the argument, sketching in his concept of the coming class war which would dominate his thinking in the future. In 1831, in his "Letter to Governor Hamilton," he openly took his stand on the side of the nullifiers and advanced nullification as the conservative or negative power of the

Constitution of a government of limited powers and sovereign states. He battled President Jackson's demand for a force bill to restore federal authority in South Carolina on the ground that it would convert the central government into one of unlimited powers. Most of all he expounded constitutional philosophy, the Constitution and law-making powers, sovereignty, the meaning of a state and the meaning of the people, earning for himself the description of "metaphysical."

J. W. Draper dismisses the whole nullification movement as nothing more than Calhoun's thwarted bitterness over the disappointment of his presidential ambitions—a scheme to divide the Union so he might become President of half.[1] David F. Houston calls this sheer misrepresentation. He does not deny that Calhoun completely reversed positions; but he does maintain that Robert J. Turnbull, in his pamphlet, The Crisis, *asserted the "first formulation of the nullification doctrine, Calhoun afterwards borrowing some of his precise phraseology." Despite his "remarkably strong individuality," Houston contends that "it would be much nearer the truth to say that South Carolina coerced Calhoun, than to say that Calhoun misguided South Carolina."* [2]

South Carolina had bitterly rebuked the Hartford Convention which had restated the doctrine. Langdon Cheves, the most nationally known Carolinian next to Calhoun, saw the Union as a national government and had frequently said so. South Carolina had gone on record as declaring the Supreme Court to be the arbiter of constitutional disputes, and the belief was widely held in South Carolina that both the general government and the states were sovereign in their separate spheres.

This did not deny that South Carolina had a right to complain or that South Carolina was on the economic decline with huge numbers of its population moving west. No one seemed to see or to want to see that slavery "was the fundamental factor," [3] *that it fixed the South upon one basic commodity whose price was now falling; that it prevented the introduction of manufacturing; and that, most of all, "slavery was in itself an economic evil." All South Carolina and its leaders seemed to see was that the state's wealth was being extorted by an unjust tariff. Calhoun*

[1] J. W. Draper, *History of the American Civil War* (New York, 1867–70).
[2] David F. Houston, *A Critical Study of Nullification in South Carolina* (New York, 1896), p. 64.
[3] Houston, p. 48.

himself was acutely aware that if the doctrine were enforced to battle the tariff today, it could be invoked to battle abolitionism tomorrow.

THE SOUTH CAROLINA EXPOSITION AND PROTEST [4]

We are the serfs of the system,—out of whose labor is raised, not only the money paid into the Treasury, but the funds out of which are drawn the rich rewards of the manufacturer and his associates in interest. Their encouragement is our discouragement. The duty on imports, which is mainly paid out of our labor, gives them the means of selling to us at a higher price; while we cannot, to compensate the loss, dispose of our products at the least advance. It is then, indeed, not a subject of wonder, when understood, that our section of the country, though helped by a kind Providence with a genial sun and prolific soil, from which spring the richest products, should languish in poverty and sink into decay, while the rest of the Union, though less fortunate in natural advantages, are flourishing in unexampled prosperity. The assertion, that the encouragement of the industry of the manufacturing States is, in fact, discouragement to ours, was not made without due deliberation. It is susceptible of the clearest proof. We cultivate certain great staples for the supply of the general market of the world:—They manufacture almost exclusively for the home market. Their object in the Tariff is to keep down foreign competition, in order to obtain a monopoly of the domestic market. The effect on us is, to compel us to purchase at a higher price, both what we obtain from them and from others, without receiving a correspondent increase in the price of what we sell. . . . The case, then, fairly stated between us and the manufacturing States is, that the Tariff gives them a protection against foreign competition in our own market, by diminishing, in the same proportion, our capacity to compete.

* * *

The committee deemed it more satisfactory to present the operation of the system on the staple States generally, than its peculiar operation on this. In fact, they had not the data, had they felt the inclination, to distinguish the oppression under which this State labors, from that of the others. It may, however, be truly said, that we are among the greatest sufferers. No portion of the world, in proportion to

[4] From "The South Carolina Exposition and Protest" (December, 1828), Crallé, ed., *Works*, VI, 10–11, 24–25, 26, 36–37.

population and wealth, ever exchanged with other countries a greater amount of its products. With the proceeds of the sales of a few great staples we purchase almost all our supplies; and that system must, indeed, act with the desolation of a famine on such a people, where the Government exacts a tax of nearly fifty per cent on so large a proportion of their exchanges, in order that a portion of their fellow-citizens might, in effect, lay one as high on the residue.

* * *

The system has not been sufficiently long in operation with us, to display its real character in reference to the point now under discussion. To understand its ultimate tendency, in distributing the wealth of society among the several classes, we must turn our eyes to Europe, where it has been in action for centuries,—and operated as one among the efficient causes of that great inequality of property which prevails in most European countries. No system can be more efficient to rear up a moneyed aristocracy. Its tendency is, to make the poor poorer, and the rich richer. Heretofore, in our country; this tendency has displayed itself principally in its effects, as regards the different sections,—but the time will come when it will produce the same results between the several classes in the manufacturing States. After we are exhausted, the contest will be between the capitalists and operatives; for into these two classes it must, ultimately, divide society. The issue of the struggle here must be the same as it has been in Europe. Under the operation of the system, wages must sink more rapidly than the prices of the necessaries of life, till the operatives will be reduced to the lowest point,—when the portion of the products of their labor left to them will be barely sufficient to preserve existence. For the present, the pressure of the system is on our section. Its effects on the staple States produce almost universal suffering. In the meantime, an opposite state of things exists in the manufacturing States. For the present, every interest among them,—except that of foreign trade and navigation, flourishes.

* * *

Our system consists of two distinct and independent Governments. The general powers, expressly delegated to the General Government, are subject to its sole and separate control; and the States cannot, without violating the constitutional compact, interpose their authority to check, or in any manner to counteract its movements, so long as they are confined to the proper sphere. So, also, the peculiar and local powers reserved to the States are subject to their exclusive control;

nor can the General Government interfere, in any manner, with them, without violating the Constitution.

In order to have a full and clear conception of our institutions, it will be proper to remark that there is, in our system, a striking distinction between *Government* and *Sovereignty*. The separate governments of the several States are vested in their Legislative, Executive, and Judicial Departments; while the sovereignty resides in the people of the States respectively. The powers of the General Government are also vested in its Legislative, Executive, and Judicial Departments, while the sovereignty resides in the people of the several States who created it. But, by an express provision of the Constitution, it may be amended or changed by three-fourths of the States; and thus each State, by assenting to the Constitution with this provision, has modified its original right as a sovereign, of making its individual consent necessary to any change in its political condition; and, by becoming a member of the Union, has placed this important power in the hands of three-fourths of the States,—in whom the highest power known to the Constitution actually resides. Not the least portion of this high sovereign authority resides in Congress, or any of the departments of the General Government. They are but the creatures of the Constitution, and are appointed but to execute its provisions; and, therefore, any attempt by all, or any of these departments, to exercise any power which, in its consequences, may alter the nature of the instrument, or change the condition of the parties to it, would be an act of usurpation.

It is thus that our political system, resting on the great principle involved in the recognized diversity of geographical interests in the community, has, in theory, with admirable sagacity, provided the most efficient check against their dangers. Looking to facts, the Constitution has formed the States into a community only to the extent of their common interests; leaving them distinct and independent communities as to all other interests, and drawing the line of separation with consummate skill, as before stated.

TO GENERAL HAMILTON ON THE SUBJECT OF STATE INTERPOSITION [5]

The formation and adoption of the Constitution are events so recent, and all the connected facts so fully attested, that it would seem

[5] From a letter "To General Hamilton on the Subject of State Interposition" (August 28, 1832), Crallé, ed., *Works*, VI, 145–47, 168–69.

impossible that there should be the least uncertainty in relation to them; and yet, judging by what is constantly heard and seen, there are few subjects on which the public opinion is more confused. The most indefinite expressions are habitually used in speaking of them. Sometimes it is said that the Constitution was made by the States, and at others, as if in contradistinction, by the people, without distinguishing between the two very different meanings which may be attached to those general expressions. . . . If by the people be meant the people collectively, and not the people of the several States taken separately; and if it be true, indeed, that the Constitution is the work of the American people collectively; if it originated with them, and derives its authority from their will, then there is an end of the argument. This right claimed for a State of defending her reserved powers against the General Government, would be an absurdity. . . . But, fortunately, the supposition is entirely destitute of truth. So far from the Constitution being the work of the American people collectively, no such political body either now or ever did exist. In that character the people of this country never performed a single political act. . . .

*   *   *

Secession is a *withdrawal from the Union;* a separation from *partners,* and, as far as depends on the member withdrawing, a *dissolution* of the partnership. It presupposes an association; a union of several States or individuals for a common object. Wherever these exist, secession may; and where they do not, it cannot. Nullification, on the contrary, *presupposes the relation of* principal and agent: the one granting a power to be executed,—the other, appointed by him with authority to execute it; *and is simply a declaration on the part of the principal, made in due form, that an act of the agent transcending his power is null and void.* It is a right belonging exclusively to the relation between principal and agent, to be found *wherever it exists, and in all its forms,* between several, or an association of principals, and their joint agents, as well as between a single principal and his agent.

The difference in their object is no less striking than in their nature. The object of secession . . . *is the dissolution of the association or union,* as far as it is concerned. On the contrary, the object of nullification is to confine the agent within the limits of his powers, by arresting his acts transcending them, *not with the view of destroying the delegated or trust power, but to preserve it, by compelling the agent to fulfil the object for which the agency or trust was created.* . . .

*   *   *

Nullification may, indeed, be succeeded by secession. In the case stated, should the other members undertake to grant the power nullified, and should the nature of the power be such as to *defeat the object of the association or union,* at least as far as the member nullifying is concerned, it would then become an abuse of power on the part of the principals, and thus present a case where secession would apply; but in no other could it be justified, except it be for a failure of the association or union to effect the object for which it was created, independent of any abuse of power.

ON THE REVENUE COLLECTION BILL [6]

Calhoun was violently opposed to the Force Bill, President Andrew Jackson's call for powder and shot to put down nullification and enforce the tariff act in South Carolina. For two days he fought "The Bloody Bill" in the Senate and was forcefully answered by Daniel Webster, who attacked not the Force Bill, but nullification, on purely constitutional grounds. Calhoun responded in kind, using Webster's own words against him in the contention that the Constitution was "a compact." The following year Calhoun delivered another attack on the Force Bill, taking the ground that our "beautiful system, with all its various, separate, and independent parts," was never intended to be consolidated in a government "of an absolute and despotic majority."

Mr. President:—I know not which is most objectionable, the provisions of the bill, or the temper in which its adoption has been urged. If the extraordinary powers with which the bill proposes to clothe the Executive, to the utter prostration of the constitution and the rights of the States, be calculated to impress our minds with alarm at the rapid progress of despotism in our country; the zeal with which every circumstance calculated to misrepresent or exaggerate the conduct of Carolina in the controversy, is seized on with a view to excite hostility against her, but too plainly indicates the deep decay of that brotherly feeling which once existed between these States, and to

[6] From speech "On the Revenue Collection Bill" (February 15 and 16, 1833), Crallé, ed., *Works*, II, 197, 222, 226–27, 228, 231–32, 234–35.

which we are indebted for our beautiful federal system, and by the continuance of which alone it can be preserved. It is not my intention to advert to all these misrepresentations; but there are some so well calculated to mislead the mind as to the real character of the controversy, and to hold up the State in a light so odious, that I do not feel myself justified in permitting them to pass unnoticed.

Among them, one of the most prominent is, the false statement that the object of South Carolina is to exempt herself from her share of the public burdens, while she participates in the advantages of the Government. If the charge were true—if the State were capable of being actuated by such low and unworthy motives, mother as I consider her, I would not stand up on this floor to vindicate her conduct.

* * *

It has been further objected, that the State has acted precipitately. What! precipitately! after making a strenuous resistance for twelve years—by essays in all forms—by resolutions, remonstrances, and protests on the part of her legislature—and, finally, by attempting an appeal to the judicial power of the United States? I say attempting, for they have been prevented from bringing the question fairly before the court, and that by an act of that very majority in Congress who now upbraid them for not making that appeal; of that majority who, on a motion of one of the members in the other House from South Carolina, refused to give to the act of 1828 its true title—that it was a *protective,* and not a *revenue* act. The State has never, it is true, relied upon that tribunal, the Supreme Court, to vindicate its reserved rights; yet they have always considered it as an auxiliary means of defence, of which they would gladly have availed themselves to test the constitutionality of protection, had they not been deprived of the means of doing so by the act of the majority.

* * *

In fact, the advocates of this bill refute their own argument. They tell us that the ordinance is unconstitutional; that it infracts the constitution of South Carolina, although, to me, the objection appears absurd, as it was adopted by the very authority which adopted the constitution itself. They also tell us that the Supreme Court is the appointed arbiter of all controversies between a state and the General Government. Why, then, do they not leave this controversy to that tribunal? Why do they not confide to them the abrogation of the ordinance, and the laws made in pursuance of it, and the assertion of that supremacy which they claim for the laws of Congress? The State stands pledged to resist no process of the court. Why, then, confer on the President the extensive and unlimited powers provided in this bill? Why authorize him to use military force to arrest the civil process of the State? But one answer can be given: That, in a contest between the State and the General Government, if the resistance be limited on both sides to the civil process, the State, by its inherent sovereignty, standing upon its reserved powers, will prove too powerful in such a controversy, and must triumph over the Federal Government, sustained by its delegated and limited authority; and in this answer we have an acknowledgment of the truth of those great principles for which the State has so firmly and nobly contended.

Having made these remarks, the great question is now presented, Has Congress the right to pass this bill? which I will next proceed to consider. The decision of this question involves an inquiry into the provisions of the bill. What are they? It puts at the disposal of the President the army and navy, and the entire militia of the country; it enables him, at his pleasure, to subject every man in the United States, not exempt from militia duty, to martial law; to call him from his ordinary occupation to the field, and under the penalty of fine and imprisonment, inflicted by a court martial, to imbrue his hand in his brother's blood.

* * *

This bill proceeds on the ground that the entire sovereignty of this country belongs to the American people, as forming one great community, and regards the States as mere fractions or counties, and not as integral parts of the Union; having no more right to resist the encroachments of the Government than a county as to resist the authority of a State; and treating such resistance as the lawless acts of so many individuals, without possessing sovereignty or political rights.

* * *

Sovereignty is by its nature indivisible. It is the supreme power in a State, and we might just as well speak of half a square, or half of a triangle, as of half a sovereignty. It is a gross error to confound the *exercise* of sovereign powers with *sovereignty* itself, or the *delegation* of such powers with the *surrender* of them. A sovereign may delegate his powers to be exercised by as many agents as he may think proper, under such conditions and with such limitations as he may impose; but to surrender any portion of his sovereignty to another is to annihilate the whole. The Senator from Delaware (Mr. Clayton) calls this metaphysical reasoning, which he says he cannot comprehend. If by metaphysics he means that scholastic refinement which makes distinctions without difference, no one can hold it in more utter contempt than I do; but if, on the contrary, he means the power of analysis and combination—that power which reduces the most complex idea into its elements, which traces causes to their first principle, and, by the power of generalization and combination, unites the whole in one harmonious system—then, so far from deserving contempt, it is the highest attribute of the human mind. It is the power which raises man above the brute—which distinguishes his faculties from mere sagacity, which he holds in common with inferior animals. It is this power which has raised the astronomer from being a mere gazer at the stars to the high intellectual eminence of a Newton or a Laplace, and astronomy itself from a mere observation of insulated facts into that noble science which displays to our admiration the system of the universe. And shall this high power of the mind, which has effected such wonders when directed to the laws which control the material world, be for ever prohibited, under a senseless cry of metaphysics, from being applied to the high purpose of political science and legislation? I hold them to be subject to laws as fixed as matter itself, and to be as fit a subject for the application of the highest intellectual power.

* * *

We are told that the Union must be preserved, without regard to the means. And how is it proposed to preserve the Union? By force! Does any man in his senses believe that this beautiful structure—this harmonious aggregate of States, produced by the joint consent of all—can be preserved by force? Its very introduction will be certain destruction to this Federal Union. No, no. You cannot keep the States united in their constitutional and federal bonds by force. Force may, indeed, hold the parts together, but such union would be the bond between master and slave—a union of exaction on one side and of unqualified *obedience* on the other. . . . Yes, exaction on the side of the master; for this very bill is intended to collect what can be no longer called taxes—the voluntary contribution of a free people—but tribute—tribute to be collected under the mouths of the cannon! . . .

. . . Disguise it as you may, the controversy is one between power and liberty; and I tell the gentlemen who are opposed to me, that, as strong as may be the love of power on their side, the love of liberty is still stronger on ours.

4

The Battle Over Abolition Petitions

The most unquestionable right may be rendered doubtful, if once admitted to be a subject of controversy.

—CALHOUN

Calhoun, as he said, believed in meeting the enemy on the frontier, in not leaving vital questions to those "who are to come after us." The first organized defiance of the slave interests resulted from the petitions from Negroes and abolitionists beseeching the end of slavery, which Calhoun saw as a "right" guaranteed by the Constitution. Through his efforts, Congress passed the "Gag Rule," which automatically tabled abolition petitions without debate. After years of effort by old Congressman John Quincy Adams, the Gag Rule was finally rescinded.

ON THE ABOLITION PETITIONS [1]

Of all the rights belonging to a deliberative body, I know of none more universal, or indispensable to a proper performance of its functions, than the right to determine at its discretion what it shall receive, over what it shall extend its jurisdiction, and to what it shall direct its deliberation and action. It is the first and universal law of all such bodies, and extends not only to petitions, but to reports, to bills, and resolutions, varied only, in the two latter, in the form of the question . . . with deliberative bodies; deprive them of the essential and primary right to determine at their pleasure what to receive or reject, and they would become the passive receptacles, indifferently, of all that is frivolous, absurd, unconstitutional, immoral, and impious, as well as what may properly demand their deliberation

[1] From speech "On the Abolition Petitions" (March 9, 1836), Crallé, ed., *Works*, II, 480–81, 482, 483–84, 486, 488–89.

43

and action. Establish this monstrous, this impious principle (as it would prove to be in practice), and what must be the consequence? To what would we commit ourselves? If a petition should be presented, praying the abolition of the constitution (which we are all bound by our oaths to protect), according to this abominable doctrine, it must be received. So if it prayed the abolition of the Decalogue, or of the Bible itself. I go further. If the abolition societies should be converted into a body of atheists, and should ask the passage of a law denying the existence of the Almighty Being above us, the Creator of all, according to this blasphemous doctrine, we would be bound to receive the petition—to take jurisdiction of it.

* * *

No one can believe that the fanatics, who have flooded this and the other House with their petitions, entertain the slightest hope that Congress would pass a law, *at this time,* to abolish slavery in this District. Infatuated as they are, they must see that public opinion at the North is not yet prepared for so decisive a step, and that seriously to attempt it now would be fatal to their cause. What, then, do they hope? What, but that Congress should take jurisdiction of the subject of abolishing slavery—should throw open to the abolitionists the halls of legislation, and enable them to establish a permanent position within their walls, from which hereafter to carry on their operations against the institutions of the slaveholding States? If we receive this petition, all these advantages will be realized to them to the fullest extent.

* * *

The Senators from the slaveholding States, who, most unfortunately, have committed themselves to vote for receiving these incendiary petitions, tell us that whenever the attempt shall be made to abolish slavery they will join with us to repel it. I doubt not the sincerity of their declaration. We all have a common interest, and they cannot betray ours without betraying, at the same time, their own. But I announce to them that they are now called on to redeem their pledge. *The attempt is now being made.* The work is going on daily and hourly. The war is waged, not only in the most dangerous manner, but in the only manner that it can be waged. Do they expect that the abolitionists will resort to arms, and commence a crusade to liberate our slaves by force? Is this what they mean when they speak of the attempt to abolish slavery? If so, let me tell our friends of the South who differ from us, that the war which the abolitionists wage against us is of a very different character, and far more effective. It is a war of religious and political fanaticism, mingled, on the part of the leaders, with ambition and the love of notoriety—and waged, not against our lives, but our character. The object is to humble and debase us in our own estimation, and that of the world in general; to blast our reputation, while they overthrow our domestic institutions. This is the mode in which they are attempting abolition, with such ample means and untiring industry; and *now is the time* for all who are opposed to them to meet the attack. How can it be successfully met? This is the important question. There is but one way: we must meet the enemy on the frontier—on the question of receiving; we must secure that important pass—it is our Thermopylae.

* * *

If to maintain our rights must increase the abolitionists, be it so. I would at no period make the least sacrifice of principle for any temporary advantage, and much less at the present. If there must be an issue, now is our time. We never can be more united or better prepared for the struggle; and I, for one, would much rather meet the danger now, than turn it over to those who are to come after us.

* * *

We love and cherish the Union; we remember with the kindest feelings our common origin, with pride our common achievements, and fondly anticipate the common greatness and glory that seem to await us; but origin, achievements, and anticipation of coming greatness are to us as nothing, compared to this question. It is to us a vital question. It involves not only our liberty, but, what is greater (if to freemen any thing can be), existence itself. The relation which now exists between the two races in the slaveholding States has existed for two centuries. It has grown with our growth, and strengthened with our strength. It has entered into and modified all our institutions, civil and political. None other can be substituted. We will not, cannot permit it to be destroyed. . . . Come what will, should it cost every drop of blood, and every cent of property, we must defend ourselves; and if compelled, we would stand justified by all laws, human and divine.

If I feel alarm, it is not for ourselves, but the Union, and the institutions of the country—to which I have ever been devotedly attached, however calumniated and slandered. Few have made greater sacrifices to maintain them, and no one is more anxious to perpetuate them to the latest generation; but they can and ought to be perpetuated only on the condition that they fulfil the great objects for which they were created—the liberty and protection of these States.

* * *

With these impressions, I ask neither sympathy nor compassion for the slaveholding States. We can take care of ourselves. It is not we, but the Union which is in danger.

ON THE RECEPTION OF ABOLITION PETITIONS [2]

As widely as this incendiary spirit has spread, it has not yet infected this body, or the great mass of the intelligent and business portion of the North; but unless it be speedily stopped, it will spread and work upwards till it brings the two great sections of the Union into deadly conflict. This is not a new impression with me. Several years since, in a discussion with one of the Senators from Massachusetts (Mr. Webster), before this fell spirit had showed itself, I then predicted that the doctrine of the proclamation and the Force Bill,—that this Government had a right, in the last resort, to determine the extent of its own powers, and enforce its decision at the point of the bayonet, which was so warmly maintained by that Senator, would at no distant day arouse the dormant spirit of abolitionism. I told him that the doctrine was tantamount to the assumption of unlimited power on the part of the Government, and that such would be the impression on the public mind in a large portion of the Union. The consequence would be inevitable. A large portion of the Northern States believed slavery to be a sin, and would consider it as an obligation of conscience to abolish it if they should feel themselves in any degree responsible for its continuance,—and that this doctrine would necessarily lead to the belief of such responsibility. . . .

. . . They who imagine that the spirit now abroad in the North, will die away of itself without a shock or convulsion, have formed a very inadequate conception of its real character; it will continue to rise and spread, unless prompt and efficient measures to stay its progress be adopted. Already it has taken possession of the pulpit, of the schools, and, to a considerable extent, of the press; those great instruments by which the mind of the rising generation will be formed.

However sound the great body of the non-slaveholding States are at present, in the course of a few years they will be succeeded by those

[2] From speech "On the Reception of Abolition Petitions" (February 6, 1837), Crallé, ed., *Works*, II, 628, 629–30, 631.

who will have been taught to hate the people and institutions of nearly one-half of this Union, with a hatred more deadly than one hostile nation ever entertained towards another. It is easy to see the end. By the necessary course of events, if left to themselves, we must become, finally, two people. It is impossible under the deadly hatred which must spring up between the two great sections, if the present causes are permitted to operate unchecked, that we should continue under the same political system. The conflicting elements would burst the Union asunder, powerful as are the links which hold it together. Abolition and the Union cannot coexist. As the friend of the Union I openly proclaim it,—and the sooner it is known the better. The former may now be controlled, but in a short time it will be beyond the power of man to arrest the course of events. We of the South will not, cannot surrender our institutions. To maintain the existing relations between the two races, inhabiting that section of the Union, is indispensable to the peace and happiness of both. It cannot be subverted without drenching the country in blood, and extirpating one or the other of the races. Be it good or bad, it has grown up with our society and institutions, and is so interwoven with them, that to destroy it would be to destroy us as a people.

* * *

But I take higher ground. I hold that in the present state of civilization, where two races of different origin, and distinguished by color, and other physical differences, as well as intellectual, are brought together, the relation now existing in the slaveholding States between the two, is, instead of an evil, a good—a positive good. I feel myself called upon to speak freely upon the subject where the honor and interests of those I represent are involved.

5
Slavery and Disunion

*The day that the balance between two sections of the coun-
try—the slaveholding states and the non-slaveholding states
—is destroyed, is a day that will not be far removed from
political revolution, anarchy, civil war, and widespread disaster.*

—Calhoun

*Slavery is a domestic institution. It belongs to the states,
each for itself to decide, whether it shall be established or
not; and if it be established, whether it should be abolished
or not.*

—Calhoun

*The defense of slavery was the burden and the tragedy
of Calhoun's last years. Fully aware that the question, if agitated,
would disrupt the Union, he spoke to silence speech, to quell
dissent, hammering down always on his conviction that the federal government had no right to limit the spread of the "peculiar
domestic institution." He somberly foresaw civil war and the
social revolution that was to occur after emancipation. He struggled to reconcile irreconcilables, to preserve the slavery which
he saw as essential to the South, and to preserve the Union
which he loved to the end—for the word "disunion" he would
never speak. Convinced that only united determination on the
part of the South would halt the determination of the North,
he drew up a "Southern Address" outlining the constitutional
"right" of slavery, which, however, many Southern congresmen
would not sign. He was too weak to deliver his last great speech,
which laid down, for all practical purposes, an ultimatum. The
Union had been rent to the breaking point; unless the North
desisted from its "aggressions," the South would be compelled
to secede.*

ON STATES' RIGHTS[1]

Looking, then, to the approaching struggle, I take my stand immovably. *I am a conservative in its broadest and fullest sense,* and such *I shall ever remain, unless, indeed, the Government shall become so corrupt and disordered, that nothing short of revolution can reform it.* I solemnly believe that our political system is, in its purity, not only the best that ever was formed, but the best possible that can be devised for us. It is the only one by which free States, so populous and wealthy, and occupying so vast an extent of territory, can preserve their liberty. Thus thinking, I cannot hope for a better. Having no hope of a better, I am a conservative; and *because I am a conservative, I am a State Rights man.* I believe that in the rights of the States are to be found the only effectual means of checking the overaction of this Government; to resist its tendency to concentrate all power here, and to prevent a departure from the constitution; or, in case of one, to restore the Government to its original simplicity and purity. State interposition, or, to express it more fully, the right of a State to interpose her sovereign voice as one of the parties to our constitutional compact, against the encroachments of this Government, is the only means of sufficient potency to effect all this; and I am, therefore, its advocate. . . .

Yet, while I thus openly avow myself a conservative, God forbid I should ever deny the glorious right of rebellion and revolution. Should corruption and oppression become intolerable, and not otherwise be thrown off—if liberty must perish, or the government be overthrown, I would not hesitate, at the hazard of life, to resort to revolution, and to tear down a corrupt government that could neither be reformed nor borne by freemen. But I trust in God things will never come to that pass.

ENGLAND AS THE GREATEST SLAVEHOLDER[2]

It would require . . . no small share of effrontery, for a nation which has been the greatest slave dealer on earth . . . to turn round

[1] From "Speech on the same subject" (January 5, 1837), Crallé, ed., *Works,* I, 614–15.

[2] From speech "On his Resolution in Respect to the Brig Enterprise" (March 3, 1840), Crallé, ed., *Works,* III, 476–79.

and declare that she neither had, nor could have the right to the property she sold us, nor could we, without deep crime, retain possession. We all know what such conduct would be called among individuals, unless, indeed, followed by a tender back of the purchase money, with an ample compensation for damages; and there is no good reason why it should be called by a less harsh epithet, when applied to the conduct of nations. . . .

Yes, she who refused to compensate our citizens for property unjustly seized and detained under her authority, on the ground that she had forbidden the recognition of slavery in her territory, had then, and has, at this day, hundreds of thousands of slaves in the most wretched condition, held by her subjects in her Eastern possessions— and worse, by herself. With all her boast she is a slaveholder, and hires out and receives hire for slaves.

*   *   *

The whole of Hindostan, with the adjacent possessions, is one magnificent plantation, peopled by more than one hundred millions of slaves, belonging to a company of gentlemen in England, called the East India Company, whose power is far more unlimited and despotic than that of any Southern planter over his slaves—a power upheld by the sword and bayonet, exacting more and leaving less by far of the product of their labor to the subject race, than is left under our own system, with much less regard to their comfort in sickness and age. This vast system of servitude carries with itself the elements of increase: not, it is true, by the African slave trade, but by means not less inhuman; that of organizing the subject race into armies, and exhausting their strength and life in reducing all around to the same state of servitude.

But it may be said, that the East India Company is but a department of the British Government, through which it exercises its control, and holds in subjection that vast region. Be it so. I stickle not for nice distinctions. But how stands the case under this aspect? If it be contrary to the laws of nature, or nations, for man to hold man in subjection individually, is it not equally contrary for a body of men to hold another in subjection? And if that be true, is it not as much so for one nation to hold another in subjection? If man individually has an absolute right to self-government, have not men aggregated into states, or nations, an equal right? . . . Or, what right to hold . . . her numerous subject colonies, all over the globe? . . .

But I approach near home. I cross the Atlantic, passing unnoticed subjugated Ireland, with her eight millions of people and only ninety thousand voters.

RESOLUTIONS ON THE SLAVE QUESTION [3]

I am against any compromise line. Yet I would have been willing to acquiesce in a continuation of the Missouri compromise, in order to preserve, under the present trying circumstances, the peace of the country. One of the resolutions in the House, to that effect, was offered at my suggestion. I said to a friend there, "Let us not be disturbers of this Union. Abhorrent to my feelings as is that compromise line, let it be adhered to in good faith; and, if the other portions of the Union are willing to stand by it, let us not refuse to stand by it. It has kept peace for some time, and, in the present circumstances, perhaps, it would be better to be continued as it is." But it was voted down by a decided majority. It was renewed by a gentleman from a non-slaveholding State, and again voted down by a like majority.

I see my way in the constitution; I cannot in a compromise. A compromise is but an act of Congress. It may be overruled at any time. It gives us no security. But the constitution is stable. It is a rock. On it we can stand, and on it we can meet our friends from the non-slaveholding States. It is a firm and stable ground, on which we can better stand in opposition to fanaticism, than on the shifting sands of compromise.

Let us be done with compromises. Let us go back and stand upon the constitution!

Well, Sir, what if the decision of this body shall deny to us this high constitutional right, not the less clear because deduced from the entire body of the instrument, and the nature of the subject to which it relates, instead of being specially provided for? What then? I will not undertake to decide. It is a question for our constituents, the slaveholding States—a solemn and a great question. If the decision should be adverse, I trust and do believe that they will take under solemn consideration what they ought to do. I give no advice. It would be hazardous and dangerous for me to do so. But I may speak as an individual member of that section of the Union. There is my family and connections; there I drew my first breath; there are all my hopes. I am a planter—a cotton-planter. I am a Southern man

[3] From "Remarks on Presenting his Resolutions on the Slave Question" (February 19, 1847), Crallé, ed., *Works*, IV, 346–48.

and a slaveholder—a kind and a merciful one, I trust—and none the worse for being a slaveholder. I say, for one, I would rather meet any extremity upon earth than give up one inch of our equality—one inch of what belongs to us as members of this great republic! What! acknowledged inferiority! The surrender of life is nothing to sinking down into acknowledged inferiority!

ADDRESS OF THE SOUTHERN DELEGATES IN CONGRESS [4]

If the determination avowed by the North to monopolize all the territories, to the exclusion of the South, should be carried into effect, that of itself would, at no distant day, add to the North a sufficient number of States to give her three-fourths of the whole; when, under the color of an amendment of the Constitution, she would emancipate our slaves, however opposed it might be to its true intent.

* * *

To destroy the existing relation between the free and servile races at the South would lead to consequences unparalleled in history. They cannot be separated, and cannot live together in peace, or harmony, or to their mutual advantage, except in their present relation. Under any other, wretchedness, and misery, and desolation would overspread the whole South. The example of the British West Indies, as blighting as emancipation has proved to them, furnishes a very faint picture of the calamities it would bring on the South. . . .

Very different would be the circumstances under which emancipation would take place with us. If it ever should be effected, it will be through the agency of the Federal Government, controlled by the dominant power of the Northern States of the Confederacy, against the resistance and struggle of the Southern. It can then only be effected by the prostration of the white race; and that would necessarily engender the bitterest feelings of hostility between them and the North. But the reverse would be the case between the blacks of the South and the people of the North. Owing their emancipation to them, they would regard them as friends, guardians, and patrons, and center, accordingly, all their sympathy in them. The people of the North would not fail to reciprocate and to favor them, instead of the whites. Under the influence of such feelings, and impelled by fanati-

⁴ From "Address of the Southern Delegates in Congress" (January 15, 1849), Crallé, ed., *Works*, VI, 308–11.

cism and love of power, they would not stop at emancipation. Another step would be taken—to raise them to a political and social equality with their former owners, by giving them the right of voting and holding public offices under the Federal Government. We see the first step toward it in the bill already alluded to—to vest the free blacks and slaves with the right to vote on the question of emancipation in this District. *But when once raised to an equality, they would become the fast political associates of the North, acting and voting with them on all questions, and by this political union between them, holding the white race at the South in complete subjection.*

ON SLAVERY [5]

The difficulty is in the diversity of the races. So strongly drawn is the line between the two in consequence, and so strengthened by the force of habit and education, that it is impossible for them to exist together in the same community, where their numbers are so nearly equal as in the slaveholding States, under any other relation than that which now exists. Social and political equality between them is impossible. No power on earth can overcome the difficulty. The causes lie too deep in the principles of our nature to be surmounted. But, without such equality, to change the present condition of the African race, were it possible, would be but to change the form of slavery. It would make them the slaves of the community instead of the slaves of individuals, with less responsibility and interest in their welfare on the part of the community than is felt by their present masters; while it would destroy the security and independence of the European race, if the African should be permitted to continue in their changed condition within the limits of those States.

ON THE AMENDMENT TO EXTEND
THE MISSOURI COMPROMISE LINE [6]

There are diseases of the body politic, as well as our natural bodies. . . . Abolition, . . . if traced to its source, . . . will be found

[5] From "Report on the Circulation of Abolitionist Petitions" (February 4, 1836), Crallé, ed., V, 204–205.

[6] From speech "On the Amendment to Extend the Missouri Compromise Line" (August 12, 1849), Crallé, ed., *Works,* IV, 516–17.

to originate in the belief of not a small portion of the people of the North, that slavery is sinful, notwithstanding the authority of the Bible to the contrary. . . . There was a period, and that not long ago . . . when the Northern states were slaveholding communities, and extensively and profitably engaged in importing slaves into the South. It would be not a little curious and interesting to trace the causes which have led, in so short a time, to so great a change; but I forbear the attempt, because it would give a greater range than I propose to my remarks. But it is pertinent to state, that an increased attachment and devotion to liberty cannot be enumerated among them. On the contrary, the standard of liberty, instead of being raised, has been greatly lowered, with the progress of abolitionism. Before it took its rise, no people were regarded as free, who did not live under constitutional governments. With us the standard was so high, that we regarded no people as free who did not live under popular, or as it was then called, Republican Governments. Even within my recollection, it was a subject of dispute whether the English people were free, as they were governed in part by a king and an aristocracy. But now every people are called free, however despotic the government. Even if conquered and subject to the unlimited control of a foreign government, they are regarded, not as slaves, but free. Indeed, serfs are scarcely regarded as slaves, and have little of the sympathy of the abolitionists. The term slave is now restricted almost exclusively to African slavery, as it exists on this continent and its islands; and it is only in that form that it excites the sympathy, or claims the attention of abolitionists. In none other do they regard it as sinful, if they are to be judged by their acts. In their eyes, sugar, coffee, cotton, or any other article made by the conquered and enslaved Hindoos or serfs of Russia, is free made,—and that only made by enslaved Africans on this continent or its islands, is slave made. To so low a standard has freedom or liberty sunk.

ON THE SLAVERY QUESTION [7]

I have, Senators, believed from the first that the agitation of the subject of slavery would, if not prevented by some timely and effective measure, end in disunion. Entertaining this opinion, I have, on all proper occasions, endeavored to call the attention of both the two great parties which divide the country to adopt some measure to prevent so great a disaster, but without success. The agitation has

[7] From speech "On the Slavery Question" (March 4, 1850), Crallé, ed., *Works,* IV, 542, 543–44, 545, 550–51, 556–58, 559–60, 571–72, 573.

een permitted to proceed, with almost no attempt to resist it, until
t has reached a point when it can no longer be disguised or denied
hat the Union is in danger. You have thus had forced upon you the
reatest and the gravest question that can ever come under your
onsideration—How can the Union be preserved?

To give a satisfactory answer to this mighty question, it is indis-
ensable to have an accurate and thorough knowledge of the nature
nd the character of the cause by which the Union is endangered.
Vithout such knowledge it is impossible to pronounce, with any
ertainty, by what measure it can be saved; just as it would be im-
ossible for a physician to pronounce, in the case of some dangerous
isease, with any certainty, by what remedy the patient could be
aved, without similar knowledge of the nature and character of the
ause which produced it. The first question, then, presented for con-
ideration, in the investigation I propose to make, in order to obtain
uch knowledge, is—What is it that has endangered the Union?

To this question there can be but one answer,—that the immediate
ause is the almost universal discontent which pervades all the states
omposing the Southern section of the Union. This widely extended
iscontent is not of recent origin. It commenced with the agitation
f the slavery question, and has been increasing ever since. The next
question, going one step further back, is—What has caused the widely
iffused and almost universal discontent? . . .

One of the causes is, undoubtedly, to be traced to the long-continued
agitation of the slave question on the part of the North, and the
many aggressions which they have made on the rights of the South
during the time. . . .

There is another lying back of it—with which this is intimately
connected—that may be regarded as the great and primary cause.
This is to be found in the fact that the equilibrium between the two
sections, in the Government as it stood when the constitution was
ratified and the Government put in action, has been destroyed. At
that time there was nearly a perfect equilibrium between the two,
which afforded ample means to each to protect itself against the aggression of the other; but, as it now stands, one section has the
exclusive power of controlling the Government, which leaves the
other without any adequate means of protecting itself against its
encroachment and oppression.

*   *   *

The result of the whole is to give the Northern section a pre-
dominance in every department of the Government, and thereby

concentrate in it the two elements which constitute the Federal Gov-ernment,—majority of States, and a majority of their population estimated in federal numbers.

*   *   *

If the South had retained all the capital which has been extracted from her by the fiscal action of the Government; and, if it had not been excluded by the ordinance of 1787 and the Missouri compromise from the region lying between the Ohio and the Mississippi rivers, and between the Mississippi and the Rocky Mountains north of 36° 30′—it scarcely admits of a doubt, that it would have divided the emigration with the North, and by retaining her own people, would have at least equalled the North in population under the census of 1840, and probably under that about to be taken. She would also, if she had retained her equal rights in those territories, have maintained an equality in the number of States with the North, and have preserved the equilibrium between the two sections that existed at the com-mencement of the Government. The loss, then, of equilibrium is to be attributed to the action of this Government.

But while these measures were destroying the equilibrium between the two sections, the action of the Government was leading to a radical change in its character, by concentrating all the power of the system in itself. The occasion will not permit me to trace the measures by which this great change has been consummated. If it did, it would not be difficult to show that the process commenced at an early period of the Government; and that it proceeded, almost without interrup-tion, step by step, until it absorbed virtually its entire powers; but without going through the whole process to establish the fact, it may be done satisfactorily by a very short statement.

That the Government claims, and practically maintains the right to decide in the last resort, as to the extent of its powers, will scarcely be denied by any one conversant with the political history of the country. That it also claims the right to resort to force to maintain whatever power it claims, against all opposition, is equally certain. Indeed it is apparent, from what we daily hear, that this has become the prevailing and fixed opinion of a great majority of the community. Now, I ask, what limitation can possibly be placed upon the powers of a govern-ment claiming and exercising such rights? And, if none can be, how can the separate governments of the States maintain and protect the powers reserved to them by the constitution—or the people of the several States maintain those which are reserved to them, and among others, the sovereign powers by which they ordained and established,

ot only their separate State Constitutions and Governments, but also
he Constitution and Government of the United States? But, if they
ave no constitutional means of maintaining them against the right
laimed by this Government, it necessarily follows, that they hold
hem at its pleasure and discretion, and that all the powers of the
ystem are in reality concentrated in it. It also follows, that the
haracter of the Government has been changed in consequence, from
a federal republic, as it originally came from the hands of its framers,
nto a great national consolidated democracy. It has indeed, at present,
all the characteristics of the latter, and not one of the former, although
it still retains its outward form.

The result of the whole of these causes combined is—that the
North has acquired a decided ascendency over every department of
his Government, and through it a control over all the powers of the
ystem. A single section governed by the will of the numerical major-
ty, has now, in fact, the control of the Government and the entire
powers of the system. What was once a constitutional federal republic,
s now converted, in reality, into one as absolute as that of the Auto-
rat of Russia, and as despotic in its tendency as any absolute govern-
nent that ever existed.

*   *   *

It is a great mistake to suppose that disunion can be effected by a
ingle blow. The cords which bound these States together in one
ommon Union, are far too numerous and powerful for that. Disunion must be the work of time. It is only through a long process,
and successively, that the cords can be snapped, until the whole fabric
falls asunder. Already the agitation of the slavery question has snapped
ome of the most important, and has greatly weakened all the others,
as I shall proceed to show.

The cords that bind the States together are not only many, but
various in character. Some are spiritual or ecclesiastical; some political;
others social. Some appertain to the benefit conferred by the Union,
and others to the feeling of duty and obligation.

The strongest of those of a spiritual and ecclesiastical nature, consisted in the unity of the great religious denominations, all of which
originally embraced the whole Union. All these denominations, with
he exception, perhaps, of the Catholics, were organized very much
upon the principle of our political institutions. Beginning with
maller meetings, corresponding with the political divisions of the
ountry, their organization terminated in one great central assemblage,
orresponding very much with the character of Congress. . . . All this

combined contributed greatly to strengthen the bonds of the Union
The ties which held each denomination together formed a strong cor
to hold the whole Union together; but, powerful as they were, the
have not been able to resist the explosive effect of slavery agitation

The first of these cords which snapped, under its explosive force
was that of the powerful Methodist Episcopal Church. The numerou
and strong ties which held it together, are all broken, and its unit
gone. They now form separate churches; and, instead of that feelin;
of attachment and devotion to the interest of the whole church whicl
was formerly felt, they are now arrayed into two hostile bodies, en
gaged in litigation about what was formerly their common property

The next cord that snapped was that of the Baptists—one of th
largest and most respectable of the denominations. That of the Pres
byterian is not entirely snapped, but some of its strands have give
way. That of the Episcopal Church is the only one of the four grea
Protestant denominations which remains unbroken and entire.

The strongest cord, of a political character, consists of the many an
powerful ties that have held together the two great parties which have
with some modifications, existed from the beginning of the Govern
ment. They both extended to every portion of the Union, and strongl
contributed to hold all its parts together. But this powerful cord ha
fared no better than the spiritual.

*   *   *

Having now, Senators, explained what it is that endangers th
Union, and traced it to its cause, and explained its nature an
character, the question again recurs—How can the Union be saved
To this I answer, there is but one way by which it can be—and tha
is—by adopting such measures as will satisfy the states belonging to th
Southern section, that they can remain in the Union consistently witl
their honor and their safety. There is, again, only one way by whicl
this can be effected, and that is—by removing the causes by which thi
belief has been produced. Do *this,* and discontent will cease—harmon
and kind feelings between the sections be restored—and every ap
prehension of danger to the Union removed. The question, then, is—
How can this be done? But, before I undertake to answer this ques
tion, I propose to show by what the Union cannot be saved.

It cannot, then, be saved by eulogies on the Union, however splen
did or numerous. The cry of "Union, Union—the glorious Union!"
can no more prevent disunion than the cry of "Health, health—
glorious health!" on the part of the physician, can save a patien
lying dangerously ill. So long as the Union, instead of being regarde

s a protector, is regarded in the opposite character, by not much less han a majority of the States, it will be in vain to attempt to conciliate hem by pronouncing eulogies on it.

Besides this cry of Union comes commonly from those whom we annot believe to be sincere. It usually comes from our assailants. But ve cannot believe them to be sincere; for, if they loved the Union, they vould necessarily be devoted to the constitution. It made the Union, —and to destroy the constitution would be to destroy the Union.

* * *

Having now shown what cannot save the Union, I return to the question with which I commenced, How can the Union be saved? There is but one way by which it can with any certainty; and that is, by a full and final settlement, on the principle of justice, of all the questions at issue between the two sections. The South asks for justice, simple justice, and less she ought not to take. She has no compromise o offer, but the constitution; and no concession or surrender to make. She has already surrendered so much that she has little to surrender. Such a settlement would go to the root of the evil, and remove all cause of discontent, by satisfying the South, she could remain honorably and safely in the Union, and thereby restore the harmony and fraternal feelings between the sections, which existed anterior to the Missouri agitation. Nothing else can, with any certainty, finally and for ever settle the questions at issue, terminate agitation, and save the Union.

But can this be done? Yes, easily; not by the weaker party, for it can of itself do nothing—not even protect itself—but by the stronger. The North has only to will it to accomplish it—to do justice by conceding to the South an equal right in the acquired territory, and to do her duty by causing the stipulations relative to fugitive slaves to be faithfully fulfilled—to cease the agitation of the slave question, and to provide for the insertion of a provision in the Constitution, by an amendment, which will restore to the South, in substance, the power she possessed of protecting herself, before the equilibrium between the sections was destroyed by the action of this Government. There will be no difficulty in devising such a provision—one that will protect the South, and which, at the same time, will improve and strengthen the Government, instead of impairing and weakening it.

But will the North agree to this? It is for her to answer the question. But, I will say, she cannot refuse, if she has half the love of the Union which she professes to have, or without justly exposing herself to the charge that her love of power and aggrandizement is far greater than

60

PART ONE

her love of the Union. At all events, the responsibility of saving the Union rests on the North, and not on the South. The South cannot save it by any act of hers, and the North may save it without any sacrifice whatever, unless to do justice, and to perform her duties under the constitution, should be regarded by her as a sacrifice.

* * *

I have now, Senators, done my duty in expressing my opinions fully, freely, and candidly, on this solemn occasion. In doing so, I have been governed by the motives which have governed me in all the stages of the agitation of the slavery question since its commencement. I have exerted myself, during the whole period, to arrest it, with the intention of saving the Union, if it could be done; and if it could not, to save the section where it has pleased Providence to cast my lot, and which I sincerely believe has justice and the constitution on its side. Having faithfully done my duty to the best of my ability, both to the Union and my section, throughout this agitation, I shall have the consolation, let what will come, that I am free from all responsibility.

6
The Disquisition and Discourse

The necessary result, then, of the unequal fiscal action of the government is, to divide the community into two great classes; one consisting of those who, in reality, pay the taxes, and, of course, bear exclusively the burden of supporting the government; and the other, of those who are the recipients of their proceeds, through disbursements, and who are, in fact, supported by the government; or, in fewer words, to divide it into tax-payers and tax-consumers.

—CALHOUN

There is, indeed, no such community, politically speaking, as the people of the United States, regarded in the light of, and as constituting one people or nation.

—CALHOUN

It was said of Calhoun after his death that he would speak most potently from the grave. He left behind for publication two books, A Disquisition on Government *and* A Discourse on the Constitution of the United States, *in which he hoped, he said, "To lay a solid foundation for political science." They were this and more; they were among the most thorough works of political philosophy to have appeared in the United States since the publication of* The Federal Papers. *They dealt primarily with the great questions of liberty and equality in a democratic society. Calhoun analyzed the concept of progress, discussed whether our system of government was federal or national, developed in detail his theory of the concurrent majority, and debated whether we were, in truth, a government of the numerical or of the concurrent majority. His thinking was so modern that he even discussed the one man, one vote concept.*

Whatever the motivation behind the composition of these two books, whatever their meaning for slaveholders, they are still of tremendous significance. They provide a brilliant analysis of the

strengths and weaknesses of our governing system and their in-
sights into the right of minorities and the tyranny of unchecked
majority rule still have validity.

FROM A DISQUISITION ON GOVERNMENT [1]

There are two different modes in which the sense of the community may be taken; one, simply by the right of suffrage, unaided;
the other, by the right through a proper organism. Each collects the
sense of the majority. But one regards numbers only, and considers
the whole community as a unit, having but one common interest
throughout; and collects the sense of the greater number of the whole,
as that of the community. The other, on the contrary, regards interests as well as numbers;—considering the community as made up
of different and conflicting interests, as far as the action of the government is concerned; and takes the sense of each, through its majority
or appropriate organ, and the united sense of all, as the sense of the
entire community. The former of these I shall call the numerical, or
absolute majority; and the latter, the concurrent, or constitutional
majority. I call it the constitutional majority, because it is an essential
element in every constitutional government,—be its form what it may.
So great is the difference, politically speaking, between the two majorities, that they cannot be confounded, without leading to great and
fatal errors; and yet the distinction between them has been so entirely
overlooked, that when the term *majority* is used in political discus-
sions, it is applied exclusively to designate the numerical,—as if there
were no other. Until this distinction is recognized, the better understood, there will continue to be great liability to error in properly
constructing constitutional governments, especially of the popular
form, and of preserving them when properly constructed. Until then,
the latter will have a strong tendency to slide, first, into the government of the numerical majority, and, finally, into absolute government
of some other form. To show that such must be the case, and at the
same time to mark more strongly the difference between the two, in
order to guard against the danger of overlooking it, I propose to
consider the subject more at length.

The first and leading error which naturally arises from overlooking
the distinction referred to, is, to confound the numerical majority
with the people; and this so completely as to regard them as identical.
This is a consequence that necessarily results from considering the

---

[1] From *A Disquisition on Government*, Crallé, ed., *Works*, I, 28, 29, 35, 54–57.

numerical as the only majority. All admit, that a popular government, or democracy, is the government of the people; for the terms imply this. A perfect government of the kind would be one which would embrace the consent of every citizen or member of the community; but as this is impracticable, in the opinion of those who regard the numerical as the only majority, and who can perceive no other way by which the sense of the people can be taken,—they are compelled to adopt this as the only true basis of popular government, in contradistinction to governments of the aristocratical or monarchical form. Being thus constrained, they are, in the next place, forced to regard the numerical majority, as, in effect, the entire people.

* * *

The necessary consequence of taking the sense of the community by the concurrent majority is, as has been explained, to give to each interest or portion of the community a negative on the others. It is this mutual negative among its various conflicting interests, which invests each with the power of protecting itself;—and places the rights and safety of each, where only they can be securely placed, under its own guardianship. Without this there can be no systematic, peaceful, or effective resistance to the natural tendency of each to come into conflict with the others: and without this there can be no constitution. It is this negative power,—the power of preventing or arresting the action of the government,—be it called by what term it may,—veto, interposition, nullification, check, or balance of power,—which, in fact, forms the constitution. They are all but different names for the negative power.

* * *

The principle [inherent] in all communities, according to these numerous and various causes, assigns to power and liberty their proper spheres. To allow to liberty, in any case, a sphere of action more extended than this assigns, would lead to anarchy; and this, probably, in the end, to a contraction instead of an enlargement of its sphere. Liberty, then, when forced on a people unfit for it, would, instead of a blessing, be a curse; as it would, in its reaction, lead directly to anarchy,—the greatest of all curses. No people, indeed, can long enjoy more liberty than that to which their situation and advanced intelligence and morals fairly entitle them. If more than this be allowed, they must soon fall into confusion and disorder,—to be followed, if not by anarchy and despotism, by a change to a form of government more simple and absolute; and, therefore, better suited to their condition. And hence, although it may be true, that a people may not have as much liberty as they are fairly entitled to, and are capable of enjoying,—yet the reverse is unquestionably true,—that no people can long possess more than they are fairly entitled to.

Liberty, indeed, though among the greatest of blessings, is not so great as that of protection; inasmuch, as the end of the former is the progress and improvement of the race,—while that of the latter is its preservation and perpetuation. And hence, when the two come into conflict, liberty must, and ever ought, to yield to protection; as the existence of the race is of greater moment than its improvement.

It follows, from what has been stated, that it is a great and dangerous error to suppose that all people are equally entitled to liberty. It is a reward to be earned, not a blessing to be gratuitously lavished on all alike;—a reward reserved for the intelligent, the patriotic, the virtuous and deserving;—and not a boon to be bestowed on a people too ignorant, degraded, and vicious, to be capable either of appreciating or of enjoying it. Nor is it any disparagement to liberty, that such is, and ought to be the case. On the contrary, its greatest praise,—its proudest distinction is, that an all-wise Providence has reserved it, as the noblest and highest reward for the development of our faculties, moral and intellectual. A reward more appropriate than liberty could not be conferred on the deserving;—nor a punishment inflicted on the undeserving more just, than to be subject to lawless and despotic rule. This dispensation seems to be the result of some fixed law;—and every effort to disturb or defeat it, by attempting to elevate a people in the scale of liberty, above the point to which they are entitled to rise, must ever prove abortive, and end in disappointment. The progress of a people rising from a lower to a higher point in the scale of liberty, is necessarily slow;—and by attempting to precipitate, we either retard, or permanently defeat it.

There is another error, not less great and dangerous, usually associated with the one which has just been considered. I refer to the opinion, that liberty and equality are so intimately united, that liberty cannot be perfect without perfect equality.

That they are united to a certain extent,—and that equality of citizens, in the eyes of the law, is essential to liberty in a popular government, is conceded. But to go further, and make equality of *condition* essential to liberty, would be to destroy both liberty and progress. The reason is, that inequality of condition, while it is a necessary consequence of liberty, is, at the same time, indispensable to progress. In order to understand why this is so, it is necessary to bear in mind, that the main spring to progress is, the desire of individuals to better their condition; and that the strongest impulse which can be given to it is, to leave individuals free to exert themselves in the manner they may deem best for that purpose, as far at least as it can be done consistently with the ends for which government is ordained,—and to secure to all the fruits of their exertions. Now, as individuals differ greatly from each other, in intelligence, sagacity, energy, perseverance, skill, habits of industry and economy, physical power, position, and opportunity,—the necessary effect of leaving all free to exert themselves to better their condition, must be a corresponding inequality between those who may possess these qualities and advantages in a high degree, and those who may be deficient in them. The only means by which this result can be prevented are, either to impose such restrictions on the exertions of those who may possess them in a high degree, as will place them on a level with those who do not; or to deprive them of the fruits of their exertions. But to impose such restrictions on them would be destructive of liberty,—while, to deprive them of the fruits of their exertions, would be to destroy the desire of bettering their condition. It is, indeed, this inequality of condition between the front and rear ranks, in the march of progress, which gives so strong an impulse to the former to maintain their position, and to the latter to press forward into their files. This gives to progress its greatest impulse. To force the front rank back to the rear, or attempt to push forward the rear into line with the front, by the interposition of the government, would put an end to the impulse, and effectually arrest the march of progress.

These great and dangerous errors have their origin in the prevalent opinion that all men are born free and equal;—than which nothing can be more unfounded and false. It rests upon the assumption of a fact, which is contrary to universal observation, in whatever light it may be regarded.

FROM *A DISCOURSE ON THE CONSTITUTION* [2]

There is, indeed, no such community *politically* speaking, as the people of the United States, regarded in the light of, and as constituting one people or nation. There never has been any such, in any stage of their existence; and, of course, they neither could, nor ever can exercise any agency,—or have any participation in the formation of our system of government, or its administration. In all its parts,—

[2] From *A Discourse on the Constitution of the United States,* Crallé, ed., *Works,* I, 162, 118–19, 168–69, 398–99.

including the federal as well as the separate State governments, it emanated from the same source,—the people of the several States. The whole, taken together, form a federal community;—a community composed of states united by a political compact;—and not a nation composed of individuals united by, what is called, a social compact. I shall next proceed to show that it is federal, in contradistinction to a confederacy.

It differs and agrees, but in opposite respects, with a national government, and a confederacy. It differs from the former, inasmuch as it has, for its basis, a confederacy, and not a nation; and agrees with it in being a government: while it agrees with the latter, to the extent of having a confederacy for its basis. . . .

* * *

But as conclusive as these reasons are to prove that the governments of the United States is federal, in contradistinction to national, it would seem, that they have not been sufficient to prevent the opposite opinion from being entertained. Indeed, this last seems to have become the prevailing one; if we may judge from the general use of the term "national," and the almost entire disuse of that of "federal." National, is now commonly applied to "the general government of the Union," —"the federal government of these States,"—and all that appertains to them or to the Union. It seems to be forgotten that the term was repudiated by the convention, after full consideration; and that it was carefully excluded from the constitution, and the letter laying it before Congress. Even those who know all this,—and, of course, how falsely the term is applied,—have, for the most part, slided into its use without reflection. But there are not a few who so apply it, because they believe it to be a national government in fact; and among these are men of distinguished talents and standing, who have put forth all their powers of reason and eloquence, in support of the theory.

* * *

It now remains to be shown, that the government is a republic;—a republic,—or (if the expression be preferred), a constitutional democracy, in contradistinction to an absolute democracy.

It is not an uncommon impression, that the government of the United States is a government based simply on population; that numbers are its only element, and a numerical majority its only controlling power. In brief, that it is an absolute democracy. No opinion can be more erroneous. So far from being true, it is, in all the aspects in which it can be regarded, preeminently a government of the concurrent majority; with an organization, more complex and refined, indeed, but far better calculated to express the sense of the whole, (in the only mode by which this can be fully and truly done,— to wit, by ascertaining the sense of all its parts), than any government ever formed, ancient or modern. Instead of population, mere numbers, being the sole element, the numerical majority is, strictly speaking, excluded, even as one of its elements.

* * *

The relative weight of population depends as much on circumstances, as on numbers. The concentrated population of cities, for example, would ever have, under such a distribution, far more weight in the government, than the same number in the scattered and sparse population of the country. One hundred thousand individuals concentrated in a city two miles square, would have much more influence than the same number scattered over two hundred miles square. Concert of action and combination of means would be easy in the one, and almost impossible in the other; not to take into the estimate, the great control that cities have over the press, the great organ of public opinion. To distribute power, then, in proportion to population, would be, in fact, to give the control of the government, in the end, to the cities; and to subject the rural and agricultural population to that description of population which usually congregate in them,— and ultimately, to the dregs of their population. This can only be counteracted by such a distribution of power as would give to the rural and agricultural population, in some one of the two legislative bodies or departments of the government a decided preponderance. And this may be done, in most cases, by allotting an equal number of members in one of the legislative bodies to each election district; as a majority of the counties or election districts will usually have a decided majority of its population engaged in agriculture or other rural pursuits. If this should not be sufficient, in itself, to establish an equilibrium,—a maximum of representation might be established, beyond which the number allotted to each election district or city should never extend.

PART TWO

JOHN C. CALHOUN VIEWED
BY HIS CONTEMPORARIES

"Have you seen Mr. Calhoun? Do you think of leaving Washington without seeing Mr. Calhoun?" was the question invariably asked of visitors to the capital. Calhoun himself was surprised that he was the object of so much curiosity, especially among foreigners from countries where he had never been. A young German, Francis Grund, and a young Englishman, George Washington Featherstonhaugh, enjoyed Calhoun's hospitality at home. Two Englishwomen, Harriet Martineau and Sarah Maury, gave widely contrasting pictures, ten years apart. The young Mrs. Jefferson Davis succumbed to hero-worship. Calhoun captivated two young abolitionists, Congressman John Wentworth and journalist Oliver Dyer, and was even a hero to his attending physician, Abraham Venable.

7
Calhoun in Private Life

FRANCIS J. GRUND: CALHOUN AT HOME [1]

We now halted before a small house in Pennsylvania Avenue, situated not far from the Capitol. This was the temporary residence of Mr. John C. Calhoun, senator from South Carolina. If the South, in general, have a right to be proud of the great number of eminent statesmen and orators who represent its interests in Congress, South Carolina in particular may glory in Mr. Calhoun. He is a statesman, not a lawyer; and perhaps the only senator in Congress whose course of reading was strictly adapted to the high functions he was to assume.

[1] From Francis J. Grund, *Aristocracy in America*, 2 Vols. (London: Richard Bentley, 1839), II, 297–98.

When my friend and I entered the room, he was stretched on a couch, from which he rose to offer us a warm Southern welcome. He almost immediately introduced the subject of politics, in which his superiority over my friend soon reduced the latter to the situation of a mere listener.

As he was explaining his views and theories, which, contrary to the usual American practice, he did in the most concise manner, and with a degree of rapidity which required our utmost attention to follow him, his face assumed an almost supernatural expression; his dark brows were knit together, his eyes shot fire, his black hair stood on end, while on his quivering lips there hung an almost Mephistophelean scorn at the absurdity of the opposite doctrine. Then, at once, he became again all calmness, gentleness, and good-nature, laughing at the blunders of his friends and foes, and commencing a highly comical review of their absurdities.

Mr. Calhoun is, without contradiction, the greatest genius in Congress, and secretly acknowledged as such even by his most declared political enemies. His speeches are the shortest, his political views the most elevated, his delivery the most impressive of any one of his colleagues; and he adds to all these qualities the most unsparing irony. He was Vice-President at the commencement of General Jackson's administration; but subsequently joined the Whigs in order to oppose the tariff, *nullified* by his native State. Without this step, which destroyed his popularity in the North, he would, with very little opposition, have become General Jackson's successor in office. This alone proves the absurdity of the charge of unlawful ambition repeatedly brought against him. The Presidential chair of *the United States,* once within his reach, was assuredly a higher mark than the Presidency of "the *Southern* Union," the *bete noire* of the enlightened opposition.

GEORGE WASHINGTON FEATHERSTONHAUGH: "THE MOST PERFECT GENTLEMAN I EVER MET" [2]

I have travelled a great deal in the Northern States without having seen so attractive a country . . . all hill and dale with occasional delightful pellucid streams. . . . Mr. C and his family received me in the most friendly manner. A delightful room was assigned to me, and here I found myself in a charming house, amidst all the

[2] From George Washington Featherstonhaugh, *A Canoe Voyage Up the Minny Sotar,* 2 Vols. (London, 1847), II, 267–68, 270–71.

refinement and comfort that are inseparable from the condition of well-bred and honorable persons. After partaking of an excellent dinner, we adjourned for the evening to the portico, where with the aid of a guitar, accompanied by a pleasing voice, and some capital curds and cream, we prolonged a most agreeable conversation to a late hour. The air of this part of the country reminded me of that of Tuscany.

*   *   *

At dinner we had . . . a great deal of interesting conversation. What an immense difference there is in the manners of the Southern gentlemen and most of those . . . in the middle and Northern States. Here the conversation was always liberal and instructive, and seldom suggested by selfish speculations of what they might gain. . . . I observed a great solicitude here for the welfare of their slaves . . . a great deal of humanity and tenderness. . . . Mr. C cultivated both cotton and Indian corn, and was an excellent man of business. I learnt from those who knew him well, that he was a man of great punctuality in his dealings, and had never been known to run into debt or enter into wild speculation. All looked up to him as the first man in South Carolina; and many who were embarrassed in their circumstances came to him for advice. . . . He himself had no embarrassments but those political struggles he was engaged in.

Living, however, at so great a distance from the northern constituencies, it was impossible for them to be sufficiently acquainted with the sterling excellence of his character. If the purity of his private life could be as generally known in the State of New York as it is in South Carolina, no demagogues could prevent him from becoming universally popular.

HARRIET MARTINEAU: "THE CAST-IRON MAN" [3]

Our pleasantest evenings were some spent at home in a society of the highest order. Ladies, literary, fashionable, or domestic, would spend an hour with us on their way home from a dinner or to a ball. Members of Congress would repose themselves by our fireside. . . . Mr. Calhoun, the cast-iron man, who looks as if he had never been born and never could be extinguished, would come in sometimes to keep our understandings upon a painful stretch for a short while, and

[3] From Harriet Martineau, *Retrospect of Western Travel*, 2 Vols. (London and New York, 1838), I, 147–49.

leave us to take to pieces his close, rapid, theoretical, illustrated talk, and see what we could make of it. We found it usually more worth retaining as a curiosity than as either very just or useful. His speech abounds in figures, truly illustrative, if that which they illustrate were but true also. But his theologies of government (almost the only subject on which his thoughts are employed), the squarest and compactest that ever were made, are composed out of limited elements, and are not, therefore, likely to stand service very well. It is at first extremely interesting to hear Mr. Calhoun talk; and there is a never-failing evidence of power in all he says and does which commands intellectual reverence; but the admiration is too soon turned into regret, into absolute melancholy. It is impossible to resist the conviction that all this force can be at best but useless, and is but too likely to be very mischievous. His mind has long lost all power of communicating with any other. I know of no man who lives in such utter intellectual solitude. He meets men, and harangues them by the fireside as in the Senate; he is wrought like a piece of machinery, set a going vehemently by a weight, and stops while you answer; he either passes by what you say, or twists it into a suitability with what is in his head, and begins to lecture again. Of course, a mind like this can have little influence in the Senate, except by virtue, perpetually wearing out, of what it did in its less eccentric days; but its influence at home is to be dreaded. There is no hope that intellect so cast in narrow theories will accommodate itself to varying circumstances; and there is every danger that it will break up all that it can, in order to remould the materials in its own way. Mr. Calhoun is as full as ever of his nullification doctrines; and those who know the force that is in him, and his utter incapacity of modification by other minds (after having gone through as remarkable a revolution of political opinion as perhaps any man ever experienced), will no more expect repose and self-retention from him than from a volcano in full force. Relaxation is no longer in the power of his will. I never saw any one who so completely gave me the idea of possession. Half an hour's conversation with him is enough to make a necessarian of anybody. Accordingly, he is more complained of than blamed by his enemies. His moments of softness in his family, and when recurring to old college days, are hailed by all as a relief to the vehement working of the intellectual machine; a relief equally to himself and others. Those moments are as touching to the observer as tears on the face of a soldier.

One incident befell during my stay which moved everybody. A representative from South Carolina was ill, a friend of Mr. Calhoun's;

and Mr. Calhoun parted from us one day, on leaving the Capitol, to
visit this sick gentleman. The physician told Mr. Calhoun on his
entrance that his friend was dying, and could not live more than a
very few hours. A visitor, not knowing this, asked the sick man how
he was. "To judge by my own feelings," said he, "much better; but
by the countenances of my friends, not." And he begged to be told the
truth. On hearing it, he instantly beckoned Mr. Calhoun to him, and
said, "I hear they are giving you rough treatment in the Senate. Let
a dying friend implore you to guard your looks and words so as that
no undue warmth may make you appear unworthy of your principles."
"This was friendship, strong friendship," said Mr. Calhoun to me and
to many others; and it had its due effect upon him. A few days after,
Colonel Benton, a fantastic senator from Missouri, interrupted Mr.
Calhoun in a speech, for the purpose of making an attack upon him,
which would have been insufferable if it had not been too absurdly
worded to be easily made anything of. He was called to order; this
was objected to; the Senate divided upon the point of order, being
dissatisfied with the decision of the chair; in short, Mr. Calhoun sat
for two full hours hearing his veracity talked about before his speech
could proceed. He sat in stern patience, scarcely moving a muscle the
whole time; and, when it was all settled in his favour, merely observed
that his friends need not fear his being disturbed by an attack of this
nature from such a quarter, and resumed his speech at the precise
point where his argument had been broken off. It was great, and
would have satisfied the "strong friendship" of his departed comrade
if he could have been there to see it.

SARAH M. MAURY: "THIS GREAT STATESMAN" [4]

The Honourable John Caldwell Calhoun,
Member of the Senate for South Carolina.
 "A reasoning, high, immortal thing."

Calhoun is my Statesman. Through good report and through evil
report; in all his doctrines, whether upon Slavery, Free Trade, Nullification, Treasury and Currency Systems, active Annexation, or *masterly inactivity*, I hold myself his avowed and admiring disciple. If
this distinguished Statesman could be prevailed upon to visit England,

[4] From Sarah M. Maury, *The Statesmen of America* (Philadelphia, 1847), pp.
168–69, 180–84.

either in a public or in a private capacity, he would command more admiration, and attract more interest than any other man of Europe or of America. The very anomaly of his position, the curious coincidences by which he becomes the representative of interests, which, nominally at least, are in contraposition to each other, and the skill and determined fidelity with which he unites and guards each several one of these interests; preserving entire the integrity of all; these attributes together compose a character so unique, an attitude so extraordinary as to be unparalleled either in his own or in any other country of the world. To know, to understand, and to appreciate him, it is requisite rapidly to review the measures of which he is the acknowledged expounder and advocate. The champion of Free Trade; a Slaveholder and Cotton Planter; the vindicator of State Rights, and yet a firm believer in the indestructibility of the Federal Union; now the advocate of war, and now of peace; now claimed as a Whig; now revered as a Democrat; now branded as a Traitor; now worshipped as a Patriot; now assailed as a Demon; now invoked as a Demi-god; now withstanding Power, and now the people; now proudly accepting office, now as proudly spurning it; now goading the Administration, now resisting it; now counselling, now defying the Executive;—but in all changes of circumstances, all trials of patience, in smiling or in adverse fortune, ever forgetful of self, and faithful only to the inspirations of the genius and the virtue of which his name is the symbol. No vice, no folly, no frailty has soiled his nature, consumed his life, or extorted his remorse; his country has been his sole engrossing passion; loved with the devotion of a Brutus, and served with the fidelity of a Regulus; he has never wasted time; each moment has been and is employed in usefulness; his public hours in the advancement of just and wise measures of policy, and his moments of solitude in the study of all subjects which tend to elucidate those measures. Politics thus may be considered to have almost exclusively occupied the life of this great Statesman; not the sordid intrigue of partisanship, not the venal craving of place and pay, not the debasing sacrifice of honesty to popularity; his soul disdains such base employment of her faculties; nay, I question if, with all its keenness, his mind could comprehend such schemes of politics. His are not even the tactics of a state or section, nor alone those of the United States, or America: but they comprise those exalted views which, deduced from philosophy and history, and proved by practical experience, are found to constitute the true policy of all nations, and to be the universal principles of all righteous governments. . . .

He came into the Senate, in the Congress of 1845–46, to preserve the peace between the two mightiest nations of the earth; and he proved himself equal to the emergency, by his fulfillment of the trust that a nation had reposed in him.

The private position of Mr. Calhoun is as remarkable as his public station. An hereditary Slave owner, he was born and educated a ruler; he sways his people with justice and mercy, and the habitual possession of power has revealed to him the secrets of the art of Government. His gracious, princely nature, accustomed to give command without appeal, is equally accustomed to receive submission without reserve; hence his gentleness; hence his indulgence; hence his compassion; no vulgar upstart display of authority is traced in his intercourse with those who own him for their Lord. . . .

The first time I saw Mr. Calhoun was in the Senate. A western member was urging war for Oregon; Calhoun sat silent, but was visibly chafed. The first time I heard him speak, the words were words of peace and praise for England. This was the only time during the space of a month that the name of my country had been uttered except in anger,—and the voice of Calhoun was as the voice of an angel;— and for many minutes I wept, overcome by feelings which it were a vain attempt to describe. His appearance is unlike that of other men. His person is tall and thin, and I have always seen him dressed in black. His action is quick, and both in society and in the Senate very expressive. He speaks with the utmost rapidity, as if no words could convey his speed of thought; his face is all intellect, with eyes so dazzling, black, and piercing that few can stand their gaze. Sixty-four years have left their dark centre yet undimmed, and the surrounding blue liquid and pure as the eye of childhood. I have seen but one alone with eyes so beautiful. Sometimes their intense look is reading each thought of *your* bosom; sometimes they are beaming with the inspirations of his own. I *believe they give out light in the dark*. And I have often beheld them suffused with emotion, when the feelings of that ingenuous breast have been excited by honest praise, or moved by sympathy. Mr. Calhoun's general expression is that of unceasing mental activity and great decision. . . . The mouth is thin, and somewhat inclined downwards at the corners; it is the proud and melancholy lip of Dante. His complexion is bronzed by the sun of the South.

I was often at the house of Mr. Calhoun, and if I admired his public career, I honoured even more his pure and lovely private life. I have understood that one reason of his declining the mission to England, in 1845, was the indisposition of his daughter, whom he had himself attended during the arduous period that he was Secretary of State. He is adored in his family, and his manners, at all times agreeable, at home are captivating. "Would you wish me," said he, "to leave my family, to sacrifice one-tenth part of the portion of life that yet remains to me, to go to England? I have made an allotment of these years: a portion for America, a portion for my own private affairs, (for I am a planter, and cannot afford to be idle,) and a portion I have reserved for peculiar purposes connected only with myself. But convince me that my *Duty* is involved in any measure, and as that has been through life my guide, *so will I yield.*" (He is the most unpersuadable of men.)

"Mr. Calhoun," said I, speaking of America, "you are a great experiment."

"We are more," said he, "we are a great hit."

* * *

[And he added,] "We Americans are the most excitable people on earth: we have plenty to eat and to drink, so we seek war for sport, that we may exhaust ourselves and our exuberance."

"Look at the mighty Mississippi! Twenty hundred miles you may travel on his waters; go on for days and nights, and see no change; it is a valley that would contain all Europe."

On the morning after the Free Trade measures were carried in the House, I saw Mr. Calhoun for the last time. After a struggle of two and twenty years, Truth and *He* had been successful, but no personal exultation sparkled in his eye, or triumphed in his words. The measure and its great consequences alone occupied his thoughts. "And there will be no reaction," said he, "which ought always to be avoided; I have ever most carefully guarded against it."

"I refused the Mission to England, because the Peace was to be made *here*; England did not want war. I should have been of no use there; here I could do much." It is generally acknowledged that Mr. Calhoun was prevailed upon to reenter the Senate to effect this object, and that the generality of the Whigs had coalesced with his party upon this point; certain it is that they (the Whig party) voted with Mr. Calhoun during the Session of 1845–46, on every subject, Free Trade alone excepted.

"Mr. Calhoun, you are very dear to England for the sake of this peace and this Free Trade." "I did not think," he answered, "that my name was even known in England, where I myself have never been.

"The British government has exhibited the greatest wisdom, judgment, and magnanimity. Had there been the least false step on the other side—had the speeches in Parliament, or the articles in the public journals, been of an exasperating character—we could not then have arranged matters on this side as we have done. No two men could have displayed more integrity of purpose, more forbearance, and more sagacity, than Lord Aberdeen and Sir Robert Peel."

Inflexible, self-sacrificing, and proud, this extraordinary personage is akin to the great names of antiquity; his sentiments are proverbs; his forecast is prophecy. He is self-made; no external advantages have contributed to the formation of his mind and character; . . . he derived no advantages from extensive foreign travel; no thoughts nor words from the prompting of other gifted men; he has never crossed the Ocean. Simple and frank, no secrets, no mystery, exist in his presence; all that he thinks, or hopes, or observes, is expressed in unreserved and natural truthfulness; no suspicion clouds his bright mind, and his remonstrance is administered openly and directly, for he deals not in the vulgarity of calumny. He is pledged to no party: "I am the partisan of no class, nor, let me add, of either political party. I am neither of the opposition nor administration." He holds in supreme contempt all arts to obtain popularity; independence and integrity to him are of priceless worth.

VARINA HOWELL DAVIS: "A MENTAL AND MORAL ABSTRACTION" [5]

When Mr. Calhoun, with head erect, cast his eagle eyes over the crowd, I felt like rising up to do homage to a king among men. His head was long, rather than broad, the ears were placed low upon it . . . his forehead was low, steep, and beetled squarely over the most glorious pair of yellow brown shining eyes, that seemed to have a light inherent in themselves; they looked steadily out from under bushy eyebrows that made the deep sockets look still more sunken. When excited, the pupils filled the iris, and made his eyes seem black. He lowered them less than anyone I have ever seen . . . they had an almost mesmeric power.

He wore his thick hair all the same length and rather long, combed straight back from his forehead. This, with his brilliant eyes and unflinching gaze, gave his head the expression of an eagle's. His mouth was wide and straight; he rarely smiled and the firm, square chin and grave manner made a personality striking in the extreme. He was

[5] From Varina H. Davis, *Jefferson Davis: A Memoir*, 2 Vols. (New York, 1890), I, 209–14.

tall and slenderly built, quick and alert in both speech and move-ment, but mind and body were so equally and rarely adjusted to each other that no dignity could be more supreme than Mr. Calhoun's.

His voice was not musical; it was the voice of a professor of mathe-matics, and suited his didactic course admirably. He made few ges-tures, but those nervous, gentlemanly hands seemed to point the way to empire. He always appeared to me rather as a mental and moral abstraction than a politician, and it was impossible, knowing him well, to associate him with mere personal ambition. His theories and his sense of duty alone dominated him.

His language was plain to poverty . . . and seemed to argue as though alone with one man, and he a devoted patriot, who only aimed to know the right to do it with all his might. . . . The duty of a citizen to the State was his theme; the reward he offered was the consciousness of having performed it faithfully. He spoke so fast, in words so concise that the loss of one or two rendered it hard to follow him. He borrowed nothing . . . from authors of the past. It was the chart of his faith which he turned towards us . . . taking it for granted we were to sail with him; and I do not think anyone present would have hesitated then to do so. When the applause . . . subsided . . . he passed from one lady to another, saying to each a few words without a trace of gallantry; yet, though he was gray and much emaciated, the fire within made him seem hardly to have reached middle age. He devoted a little more time . . . to the wife of the orator of the evening, and his manner was so paternal and full of indulgent sympathy that I found myself telling him what a grief it was to contemplate my first separation from my mother. He spoke of a daughter named Cornelia, near my age, who loved him better than anyone else, and told some little anecdotes of her, and of his brilliant Anna . . .

. . . Thus began a friendship which lasted through his life and was attested by long letters on governmental subjects, written as though to an intellectual equal. It was one of the sources of his power over the youth of the country that he assumed nothing except a universal, honest, cointelligence between him and the world, and his conversation with a girl was on the same subjects as with a states-man.

. . . His handwriting, though it looked neat was almost indecipher-able. I once sent him back his letter to read for me, and he responded, "I know what I think on this subject but cannot decipher what I wrote."

JOHN W. WENTWORTH: "THE MOST CHARMING MAN IN CONVERSATION WHOM I EVER HEARD" [6]

This excerpt and the two following illustrate the almost hypnotic power Calhoun wielded over young men, even those opposed to him ideologically.

The next one of these four great men whom I met with at Washington was John C. Calhoun, who was appointed secretary of state in March, 1844. It was whilst the question of annexing Texas was being agitated, in which the western and southern Democrats were in sympathy. He invited me to his residence one evening, and he had me alone. He was the most charming man in conversation whom I ever heard. He spoke of Chicago very interestedly, of which he had derived considerable information through his official intercourse with the officers of Fort Dearborn whilst secretary of war, from 1817 to 1825. He spoke of the West as the natural ally of the South, and of the Mississippi and upper lakes as great inland seas deserving the same governmental consideration as the oceanic waters. He presented me with a book containing his biography and speeches, with his compliments and autograph. I wrote a narrative of the evening's conversation and pasted it in the book, but the Chicago fire has prevented me from giving you the seductive language of one who had been for many years plotting the dissolution of the Union to a young and inexperienced member of Congress. I overtook Col. Benton on my way home; and when he ascertained where I had been, and saw my book, he became extremely violent, averring that he could tell me every word that Calhoun had uttered. He said it was Mr. Calhoun's custom to early procure interviews with young men, and instill into their minds the seeds of secession, nullification, and treason.

*   *   *

Mr. Calhoun spoke like a college professor demonstrating to his class. His position was stationary, and he used no gesticulation. His pale and livid countenance indicated the cloister. His voice was silvery and attractive, but very earnest. His eyes indicated quick perception.

[6] From John W. Wentworth, *Congressional Reminiscences* (Chicago, 1882), pp. 20–25.

Starting with the most plausible premises, he would carry you irresistibly along with more plausible reasoning until you would be puzzled to know how much back-track it was indispensably necessary for you to take to avoid conclusions which would make it difficult to tell the difference between your views and those of a South Carolina secessionist. After having heard all the senators speak, if a stranger should select the one, irrespective of doctrine, who came nearest a saint, he would select Mr. Calhoun: and such he is held to be throughout most of the South to this day. College professors in the South were his great admirers, and taught his doctrines to their students. Educated clergymen and all fashionable society there lost no opportunities of manifesting their admiration of him. . . . And Mr. Calhoun's prestige was so worked up that Southern visitors, both gentlemen and ladies, were as much expected to call upon him as upon the President. At the time of his death, he was gaining a strong foothold among the scholars of the North, who seemed incapable of resisting the seductive reasoning of his perceptive, comprehensive, and analytic mind. Senator John P. Hale of New Hampshire, once came to my seat and said: "I am going to astonish you. Mr. Calhoun has just brought to me a letter, which he said he had just received from President Nathan Lord, of Dartmouth College, and asked me a great many questions about him and the college. He left me, asserting that President Lord was one of the ablest thinkers and profoundest reasoners in the country." At that time, President Lord was not only the head of the college, but of the Congregational denomination in New England. With a bravery worthy of a better cause he followed Mr. Calhoun's doctrines to their natural sequence, and he had to give up his position. No man ever exerted the influence upon this country that Mr. Calhoun did. All the calamities of the late war were the legitimate outgrowth of doctrines of which he was the father, and to which the sincerity of his devotion was manifested by his advocacy of them in his dying hour.

I have a vivid recollection of his last speech, the whole of which I heard. He came into the senate chamber, supported by two friends. Every one saw that his hours were numbered. He feebly addressed the presiding officer, and asked that Senator James M. Mason, of Virginia, be permitted to read his speech. He lingered through the whole reading, although consuming quite two hours, his eyes moving about his audience to notice its effect. Here is one of the closing passages: "If you who represent the strongest portion can not agree to settle this question upon the broad principle of justice and duty, say so, and let the States we both represent agree to separate and part in peace. If you are unwilling we should part in peace, tell us so, and we shall know what to do."

If a man of Mr. Calhoun's high position and age, standing upon the brink of eternity, could thus speak, it is easy to conjecture what would be the effect upon the younger members from the South. Senator Mason read the speech in a very haughty and defiant tone, well calculated to engender the bitterest feelings. . . .

. . . Mr. Calhoun always prided himself upon his civility, decorum, and observance of all the rules of propriety in his intercourse with his fellow men. One would not be justified in saying, from his own standpoint, that Mr. Calhoun ever did or said an uncivil thing. One day, after characterizing the effects of spreading antislavery sentiments among the slaves of the South, he said he deemed it his duty to define the rules which would govern his conduct with antislavery men. If one of them asked him a civil question, he should give him a civil answer, and nothing more. He should never originate a conversation with one of them unless in the line of unavoidable business. If one offered to him his hand, he should take it. But he should never offer his hand to one. With this idea of Mr. Calhoun, I presume, originated at the South what is called social ostracism; but all the ostracizers have not the culture and refinement that the great South Carolinian had. In my early congressional career, when I was supporting the annexation of Texas, I received a great many hearty shakes from the hand of Mr. Calhoun. But when I became an advocate of the freedom of the Mexican acquisition, I received only those shakes which I went after, knowing the terms. Mr. C.'s history shows us how very bad a very good man can be. His life was spotless, but his influence was extremely deleterious.

OLIVER DYER: "THERE WERE AT LEAST TWO CALHOUNS" [7]

Dyer's memoir was written in 1889 from shorthand notes taken forty years earlier.

The rabid abolitionists . . . of whom I was one . . . felt towards Calhoun the same as Southern men . . . felt towards William Lloyd Garrison. All through the North, Calhoun was known as the "Great Secessionist," the "Great Nullifier," the "Great Disunionist"

[7] Oliver Dyer, *Great Senators of the United States Forty Years Ago* (New York, 1889), pp. 147–52, 166, 170–72, 185–87.

nd the "Great" bad man generally. . . . His appearance satisfied me
ompletely. . . . Had I come across his likeness in a copy of Milton's
aradise Lost, I have at once accepted it . . . as a masterpiece of
ome great artist who had a peculiar genius for Satanic portraiture.
. . His features were strongly marked and their expression was firm,
tern, aggressive. . . .

His rising . . . brought the previously scattered and indifferent at-
ention of the Senate to a focus. . . . I was much impressed by the
learness of Calhoun's views, by the bell-like sweetness and resonance
f his voice, the elegance of his diction, and the exquisite courtesy of
is demeanor. Such a combination of attractive qualities was a reve-
ation to me, and I spontaneously wished that Calhoun was an Abolitionist, so we could have him talking on our side. . . . I was vexed
nd astonished at myself that such a change should have occurred in
ay feelings towards the Great Nullifier . . . as time went on the
hange also went on in spite of all that I could do.

* * *

I zealously joined in the outcry against him for years, and hated
is very name, until I became acquainted with him and the facts.

* * *

I asked Mr. Calhoun what kind of a man General Jackson was.
he effect of the question upon him made a profound impression
pon me. . . . Calhoun sank into profound quiescence. . . . Soon he
ooked at me benignly and said: "General Jackson was a great man."

The surpassingly beautiful expression of Calhoun's luminous eyes
nd the sweet, gentle tone of his voice . . . are now present with me,
s I write. . . . Why should he, a dying man, continue to hate him
ho was already dead[;] . . . the answer . . . came from . . . the
nnermost nobility of his nature. . . .

I had a genuine affection for him, and mourned over what seemed
o me to have been his political decadence. . . . No young man on this
ontinent ever started on a public career with brighter, nobler prom-
e than did that gifted, pure-souled young South Carolinian. . . .

. . . He was by all odds the most fascinating man in private inter-
ourse that I ever met. His conversational powers were marvelous.
. . His manner was simple and unpretentious. . . . His ideas were
o clear and his language so plain that he made a path of light
hrough any subject he discussed. . . .

. . . There were at least two Calhouns, perhaps there were sev-
ral[;] . . . the man himself seemed to be a different personage at

different times, according to the question or subject before him. His faculties . . . were simply a confederacy, and every one of them was a sovereign faculty, which could think and act for itself. . . . His convictions on the subject of slavery were as fixed and unchangeable as an elementary principle of nature; and, as to them, his mind was incapable of exchanging ideas with other minds. . . .

Calhoun's kindness of heart was inexhaustible. He impressed me as being deeply but unobtrusively religious, and was so morally clear and spiritually pure that it was a pleasure to have one's soul get close to his soul—a feeling that I never had for any other man. He seemed to exhale an atmosphere of purity, as fresh . . . and bracing as a breeze from the prairie, the ocean, or the mountain. . . . He was inexpressibly urbane, refined, gentle, winning; and yet he was strong and thoroughly manly with an elegant and engaging invincibleness pervading his softness and gentleness. I admired Benton; I admired Clay still more; I admired Webster, on the intellectual side, most of all, but I loved Calhoun.

ABRAHAM VENABLE: "THE ARDENT FRIEND OF THE UNION AND THE CONSTITUTION" [8]

Early in the winter of 1848–49 his failing health gave uneasiness to his friends. A severe attack of bronchitis, complicated with an affection of the heart, disqualified him for the performance of his senatorial duties with the punctuality which always distinguished him. It was then that I became intimately acquainted with his mind, and above all, with his heart. Watching by his bedside, and during his recovery, I ceased to be astonished at the power which his mastermind and elevated moral feelings had always exerted upon those who were included within the circle of his social intercourse. It was a tribute paid spontaneously to wisdom, genius, truth. Patriotism, honesty of purpose, and purity of motive, rendered active by the energies of such an intellect as hardly ever falls to any man, gathered around him sincere admirers and devoted friends. That many have failed to appreciate the value of the great truths which he uttered, or to listen to the warning which he gave, is nothing new in the history of great minds. Bacon wrote for posterity, and men of profound sagacity always think in advance of their generation. His body was sinking under the invasion of disease before I formed his acquaintance, and he was

[8] From E. P. Thomas, *The Carolina Tribute to Calhoun* (Charleston, 1857), pp. 36–37, 77.

assing from among us before I was honored with his friendship. I
witnessed with astonishment the influence of his mighty mind over
his weak physical structure. Like a powerful steam engine on a frail
bark, every revolution of the wheel tried its capacity for endurance
to the utmost. But yet his mind moved on, and, as if insensible to the
decay of bodily strength, put forth, without stint, his unequalled
powers of thought and analysis, until nature well-nigh sunk under
the imposition. His intellect preserved its vigor while his body was
sinking to decay. The menstruum retained its powers of solution,
while the frail crucible which contained it was crumbling to atoms.
During his late illness, which, with a short intermission, has continued
since the commencement of this session of Congress, there was no
abatement of his intellectual labors. They were directed as well to the
momentous questions now agitating the public mind, as to the com-
pletion of a work which embodies his thoughts on the subject of
government in general and our own Constitution in particular; thus
distinguishing his last days by the greatest effort of his mind, and
bequeathing it as his richest legacy to posterity.

Cheerful in a sick chamber, none of the gloom which usually at-
tends the progress of disease annoyed him; severe in ascertaining the
truth of conclusions, because unwilling to be deceived himself, he
scorned to deceive others; skillful in approaching the past, and im-
partial in his judgment of the present, he looked to the future as
dependent on existing causes, and fearlessly gave utterance to his
opinions of its nature and character; the philosopher and the statesman, he discarded expedients by which men "construe the times to
their necessities." He loved the truth for the truth's sake, and believed that to temporize is but to increase the evil which we seek to
remove. The approach of death brought no indication of impatience—
no cloud upon his intellect. To a friend who spoke of the time and
manner in which it was best to meet death, he remarked: "I have but
little concern about either; I desire to die in the discharge of my duty;
I have an unshaken reliance upon the providence of God."

I saw him four days after his last appearance in the Senate chamber,
gradually sinking under the power of his malady, without one mur-
mur at his affliction, always anxious for the interest of his country,
deeply absorbed in the great question which agitates the public mind,
and earnestly desiring its honorable adjustment, unchanged in the
opinions which he had held and uttered for many years, the ardent
friend of the Union and the Constitution, and seeking the perpetuity
of our institutions, by inculcating the practice of justice and the
duties of patriotism.

Aggravated symptoms, on the day before his death, gave notice (
his approaching end. I left him late at night, with but faint hopes (
amendment; and, on being summoned early the next morning,
found him sinking in the cold embrace of death; calm, collected, an
conscious of his situation, but without any symptom of alarm, h
face beaming with intelligence, without one indication of sufferin
or of pain. I watched his countenance, and the lustre of that brigh
eye remained unchanged, until the silver cord was broken, and the
it went out in instantaneous eclipse. When I removed my hand fror
closing his eyes he seemed as one who had fallen into a sweet an
refreshing slumber. Thus, sir, closed the days of JOHN CALDWEL
CALHOUN, the illustrious American statesman.

8

Calhoun in Congress

*Calhoun provided colorful and controversial "copy"
for the journalists of his day. Newspapermen like William
Mathews, E. L. Magoon, and Nathaniel P. Willis gave objective
appraisals, while abolitionists like James Russell Lowell and William Lloyd Garrison predictably damned him. Calhoun riveted
attention in Congress from his first appearance there. Thomas
Ritchie, editor of the Richmond Enquirer, compared him to
"one of the sages of the old Congress, with all the graces of
youth," and predicted that he would become "one of the master
spirits who stamp their name upon the age in which they live"
(December 24, 1811).*

*Contemporary admirers of the art of oratory were struck by
his logic, magnetism, and the complexity of his thought. His
colleague, Senator Thomas Hart Benton while considering him
"a humbug" as a man, had unlimited admiration for him as an
orator, especially for his simplicity of speech and hatred of the
trite.*

THOMAS HART BENTON: "IT WAS A MASTERLY ORATION"[1]

He did reply, and at his own good time, which was at the end
of twenty days; and in a way to show that he had "smelt the lamp,"
not of Denades, but of Demosthenes, during that time. It was pro-
foundly mediated and elaborately composed: the matter solid and
condensed; the style chaste, terse and vigorous; the narrative clear;
the logic close; the sarcasm cutting; and every word bearing upon the
object in view. It was a masterly oration, and like Mr. Clay's speech,
divided into two parts; but the second part only seemed to occupy his
feelings, and bring forth words from the heart as well as from the
head. And well it might! He was speaking, not for life, but for char-

[1] From Thomas Hart Benton, *Thirty Years' View*, 2 Vols. (New York, 1854–56),
II, 98.

85

acter! and defending public character, in the conduct which makes
it, and on high points of policy, which belonged to history—defending it before posterity and the present age, impersonated in the American Senate, before which he stood, and to whom he appealed as judges
while invoking as witnesses. He had a high occasion, and he felt it; a
high tribunal to plead before, and he rejoiced in it; a high accuser,
and he defied him; a high stake to contend for, his own reputation:
and manfully, earnestly, and powerfully did he defend it. He had
a high example both in oratory, and in the analogies of the occasion,
before him; and well had he looked into that example. I happened
to know that in this time he refreshed his reading of [Demosthenes']
"Oration on the Crown"; and, as the delivery of his speech showed,
not without profit. Besides its general cast, which was a good imi-
tation, there were passages of a vigor and terseness—of a power and
simplicity—which would recall the recollection of that masterpiece
of the oratory of the world. There were points of analogy in the cases
as well as in the speeches, each case being that of one eminent statesman accusing another, and before a national tribunal, and upon the
events of a public life. More happy than the Athenian orator, the
American statesman had no foul imputations to repel. Different from
Æschines and Demosthenes, both himself and Mr. Clay stood above
the imputation of corrupt action or motive. If they had faults, and
what public man is without them? they were the faults of lofty natures
—not of sordid souls; and they looked to the honors of their country—
not its plunder—for their fair reward.

JAMES RUSSELL LOWELL: HE "RUN[S] A TILT AT THE SPIRIT OF THE AGE" [2]

Mr. Calhoun . . . seems to think that the light of the nineteenth
century is to be put out as soon as he tinkles his little cowbell curfew.
Whenever slavery is touched, he sets up his scarecrow of dissolving
the Union. . . . Something more than a pumpkin lantern is required
to scare manifest and irretrievable Destiny out of her path. Mr. Calhoun cannot let go the apron string of the Past. . . . Mr. Calhoun
has somehow acquired the name of a great statesman, and, if it be
great statesmanship to put lance in rest and run a tilt at the Spirit
of the Age, with the certainty of being next moment hurled neck
and heels in the dust amid universal laughter, he deserves the title.

[2] From James Russell Lowell, *The Bigelow Papers* (Boston: Ticknor and Fields,
1866), pp. 63–64.

DR. WILLIAM MATHEWS: "ONE ABSORBING PASSION SEEMS TO HAVE TAKEN POSSESSION OF HIS SOUL" [3]

[Calhoun's primary power is that of analysis and] his most striking characteristic [is] the depth of his convictions . . . his willingness to stake life and honor on each sentence. No man ever cared less for the grace and polish of the schools. Intensely earnest, he cared only to make himself understood. . . . Calhoun was always dry, direct, intensely ratiocinative. . . . There is an abundance of metaphysical subtlety, of hard reasoning, and "obstinate questionings," in his speeches, but . . . none of the poetry of eloquence. . . . One absorbing passion seems to have taken possession of his soul, and to have overpowered all the rest. . . . It may be said of Calhoun, that the ideal of his life was to gather statistics of the United States, and work them up into theories of State Rights and Nullification.

[His words when] assailing an enemy, were . . . fierce, blunt, and rudely terrible. . . . Calhoun breaks your bones and leaves you sprawling on the floor.

E. L. MAGOON: "MR. CALHOUN FLAUNTS IN NO GAUDY RHETORICAL ROBES" [4]

Mr. Calhoun flaunts in no gaudy rhetorical robes of scarlet and gold, but comes into the forum clothed in the simplest garb, with firm hands grasping the reins of fancy and intent only on giving a reason for the faith that is him. . . . His language is exceedingly choice. . . . His piercing intellect is often illuminated by the brightest imagination, but this latter faculty ever contents itself with the office of ministering only to reason.

* * *

Mr. Calhoun is one of those men whom Providence sends upon earth at remote intervals, to do the chief thinking of their age, to sift the particles of truth from the "rubbish." . . . Sparing of words, but teeming with ideas, they coin great principles in the precious mentage of their mind, and hurl them into profuse and popular circulation. . . .

[3] From Dr. William Mathews in *Oratory and Orators* (Chicago, 1879), pp. 321–22.
[4] From E. L. Magoon, *Living Orators in America* (New York, 1849), pp. 223–24, 225, 226, 233.

It is a mistake to suppose that he jumps at his conclusions without due care and consideration. No man examines with more care, or with more intense labor, every question upon which his mind is called to act. The difference between him and others is, that he thinks constantly, with little or no relaxation. Hence the restless activity and energy of his mind always place him far in advance of those around him. He has reached the summit, while they have just commenced to ascend.

NATHANIEL P. WILLIS: "MR. CALHOUN LIVES IN HIS MIND" [5]

Mr. Calhoun lives in his mind and puts a sort of bathing dress value on his body. There is a temporary-looking tuckaway of his beard and hair, as if they would presently be better combed in another place—mouth and eyes kept clear, only, for a brief life-swim in the ocean of politics. His is tall, hollow-chested, and emaciated, and both face and figure are concave, with the student's bend forward. He smiles easily when spoken to—indeed with rather a simple facility— though in longer conversation, he gives his eye to the speaker, barely in recognition of an idea—with a most "verbum sap" withdrawal from talkative men. When speaking in the Senate he is a very startling looking man. His skin lies sallow and loose on the bold frame of his face—his stiff gray hair spreads off from rather a low forehead with the semicircular radiation of the smoke from a wheel of fireworks just come to a standstill—the profuse masses of white beard in his throat catch the eye like the smoulder of a fire under his chin—and his eyes, bright as coals move with jumps, as if he thought in electric leaps from one idea to another. He dresses carelessly, walks the street absent-mindedly, and is treated with the most marked personal respect and involuntary deference, by his brother senators.

[5] From Nathaniel Willis, *Hurry-Graphs* (New York, 1851), pp. 180–81.

9
Friends and Adversaries

Alive, Calhoun aroused as much controversy among his contemporaries as he was to invoke among historians after he was dead. Feelings about him ranged from Daniel Webster's unqualified admiration to Thomas Hart Benton's animosity and President James Knox Polk's contempt. The greatest surprise in all Calhoun historiography is the backhanded but profound intellectual admiration shown by his greatest adversary, the black abolitionist Frederick Douglass. Jackson viewed the South Carolinian with implacable hostility and died regretting that he had not hanged him. John Quincy Adams displayed the gamut of emotions aroused by Calhoun. Adams' early impression of him in Monroe's cabinet was of a courageous, independent thinker— "A man of fair and candid mind, of honorable principles, and of ardent patriotism. He is above all sectional and factional prejudices." [1] *Years later he regarded him as a slave-monger with a total "disregard of all moral principles."* [2] *In general, those who hated Calhoun the most, knew him personally the least. The hatreds were usually political hatreds, although the diaries of both Polk and Adams offer sufficient evidence of their capacity for believing the worst of people. As early as 1820 Calhoun had discussed with Adams the possible dissolution of the Union over slavery. This did not diminish Adams' admiration for Calhoun's "sound, judicious, and comprehensive mind," but the Southerner's "hurried ambition" to become President or Vice-President aroused the suspicions of the ambitious Adams. "Calhoun's game now," he noted in 1824, "is to unite Jackson's supporters and mine upon him for Vice-President. Look out for breakers."* [3] *Adams' worst fears were realized when Calhoun as Vice-President let the drunken Virginia Senator, John Randolph of Roanoke, harangue against the Administration for ten hours at a time. When Calhoun neatly transferred his forces into the*

[1] Charles Francis Adams, ed., *Memoirs of John Quincy Adams,* 12 Vols. (Philadelphia, 1874–77), V, 361.
[2] *Ibid.,* XII, 36.
[3] *Ibid.,* VI, 279, 273 (April, 1824).

*Jackson camp, Adams burst out—in private—against Calhoun's
"considerable talent and burning ambition; stimulated to frenzy
by success, flattery, and primitive advancement; governed by no
steady principle . . . the dupe and fool of every knave cunning
enough to drop the oil of fools in his ear." [4] Though Adams
admired the logic of nullification, he believed Calhoun to be
the instigator of the nullification troubles in South Carolina
and feared that he would divide the Union into a Northern and
Southern Confederacy. From that time on he hated him pro-
foundly.*

*Jackson, if possible, was soon to hate Calhoun even more.
Again Adams' Memoirs provide evidence that was unavailable
to the contenders. Jackson's foray into Florida in 1819 had
aroused the entire Monroe cabinet; Adams alone defended the
wayward General. Calhoun, Adams noted, though believing Jackson to be "pure and upright" was "personally offended that
Jackson had disregarded the authority of the Department," and
"bore the argument" against Adams.[5] The story got out just the
other way: Calhoun was made to appear Jackson's solitary defender, and Calhoun never disavowed that impression until the
whole house of cards toppled about his head years later. "Duplicity," roared Jackson. He left behind him after his death a paper
that showed his outrage—which Thomas Hart Benton presented
in his Thirty Years' View. "It was at the sacrifice of every principle . . . that Mr. Calhoun managed to throw all responsibility
on his political rivals . . . the mask was worn with consummate
skill. . . . Not a whisper of disapprobation or of doubt reached
me. . . . Complete and entire was the deception." Calhoun, who
had sought "a court of inquiry," had presented himself as Jackson's foremost supporter, "all smiles and politeness and perfidy." [6]*

THOMAS HART BENTON: "MORE WRONG NOW THAN EVER" [7]

*Thomas Hart Benton printed Jackson's outburst with relish.
His own animosity towards Calhoun was legendary. He did ad-*

[4] *Ibid.*, VII, 477 (February, 1828).

[5] *Ibid.*, IV, 108, 113.

[6] Thomas Hart Benton, *Thirty Years' View*, 2 Vols. (New York, 1854–56), I, 168–79.

[7] From Thomas Hart Benton, *Thirty Years' View*, 2 Vols. (New York, 1854–56), II, 648–49. The passage quoted in the introductory note appears on page 637 of the same volume.

mire Calhoun as an orator and respected his financial integrity. On the Texas negotiations he grudgingly admitted that "Mr. Calhoun had over Mr. Tyler that ascendant which it is the prerogative of genius to exercise over inferior minds." Nevertheless, on the whole question of Texas and the Mexican War that followed, Benton believed Calhoun to have been absolutely wrong.

The Senator from South Carolina has been wrong in all this business, from beginning to ending—wrong in 1819, in giving away Texas—wrong in 1836, in his sudden and hot haste to get her back—wrong in all his machinations for bringing on the Texas question of 1844—wrong in breaking up the armistice and peace negotiations between Mexico and Texas—wrong in secretly sending the army and navy to fight Mexico while we were at peace with her—wrong in secretly appointing the President of Texas president-general of the army and navy of the United States, with leave to fight them against a power with whom we were at peace—wrong in writing to Mexico that he took Texas in view of all possible consequences, meaning war —wrong in secretly offering Mexico, at the same time, ten millions of dollars to hush up the war which he had created—wrong now in refusing Mr. Polk three millions to aid in getting out of the war which he made—wrong in throwing the blame of this war of his own making upon the shoulders of Mr. Polk—wrong in his retreat and occupation line of policy—wrong in expelling old Father Ritchie from the Senate, who worked so hard for him during the Texas annexation—and more wrong now than ever, in that string of resolutions which he has laid upon the table, and in which, as Sylla saw in the young Caesar many Mariuses, so do I see in them many nullifications.

JAMES KNOX POLK: "MR. CALHOUN HAS ASPIRATIONS" [8]

James Knox Polk was suspicious from the first of John C. Calhoun. He was convinced that a desire to be President was the basis of Calhoun's every mood and motivation; as he put it, "Mr. Calhoun has aspirations." From the first, he was sure Calhoun would be in opposition to him. He saw Calhoun's proposal to settle the Oregon question on the basis of the forty-ninth

[8] From the *Diary of James Knox Polk,* reprinted through the courtesy of the Chicago Historical Society.

92

parallel (a compromise which Polk eventually accepted) as a "game to make himself President." These "peace gentlemen" had made England all the more arrogant in its demands; Calhoun had "embarrassed the administration on the Oregon question" (April 21, 1846). Polk did not see Calhoun's quiet courage in trying to cool the war fever or his concern that war would increase the centralizing tendencies already at work in the government. He grudgingly sent for Calhoun to ask his advice on the final settlement; the interview was pleasant and Calhoun in a good humor. Two months later Calhoun led the opposition to Polk's plan to send ten more regiments to Mexico and Polk pronounced him, "the most mischievous man in the Senate to my administration." What was bothering Calhoun was that he had not been continued as Secretary of State. Polk's smouldering anger burst into full flame when Calhoun, who had earlier assured Polk that he did not desire to see slavery extended, attempted to rally the Southern senators on the slave question.

[Calhoun is] desperate in his aspirations to the Presidency, . . . unpatriotic [and] wicked. . . . I now entertain a worse opinion of Mr. Calhoun than I have ever done before. He is wholly selfish, and I am satisfied has no patriotism. A few years ago he was the author of Nullification and threatened to dissolve the Union on account of the tariff . . . he selects slavery upon which to agitate the country . . . the Constitution settles these questions.

DANIEL WEBSTER: "MUCH THE ABLEST MAN IN THE SENATE" [9]

Although at odds politically, Daniel Webster and John C. Calhoun had tremendous personal admiration for each other. In part, the esteem was intellectual; Webster was one of the few men of his time who had some understanding of Calhoun's solitary intellect and he gave Calhoun the comfort of knowing that there was at least one person who comprehended what he was trying to say. Webster always watched the display of Calhoun's talents in debate "with pleasure, often with much instruction, not infrequently with the highest degree of admi-

[9] From *Obituary Addresses* (Washington, D.C.: John T. Towers, 1850), pp. 24–27.

ration." He told his biographer, Peter Harvey, that Calhoun was "long-headed, a man of extraordinary power,—much the ablest man in the Senate, in fact, the greatest man that he had known through his entire public life." Whatever their differences, there always existed between them "a great deal of personal kindness." Webster visited the dying Calhoun in March, 1850. Calhoun summoned his last strength to hear Webster's great speech on March 7, and the realization that his friend had risen from what he believed to be his deathbed to hear him moved Webster to tears.

Mr. Calhoun was calculated to be a leader in whatsoever association of political friends he was thrown. He was a man of undoubted genius, and of commanding talent. All the country and all the world admit that. His mind was both perceptive and vigorous. It was clear, quick, and strong.

Sir, the eloquence of Mr. Calhoun, or the manner of his exhibition of his sentiments in public bodies, was part of his intellectual character. It grew out of the qualities of his mind. It was plain, strong, terse, condensed, concise; sometimes impassioned—still always severe. Rejecting ornament, not often seeking far for illustration, his power consisted in the plainness of his propositions, in the closeness of his logic, and in the earnestness and energy of his manner. These are the qualities, as I think, which have enabled him through such a long course of years to speak often, and yet always command attention. His demeanor as a Senator is known to us all—is appreciated, venerated by us all. No man was more respectful to others; no man carried himself with greater decorum, no man with superior dignity. I think there is not one of us but felt when he last addressed us from his seat in the Senate, his form still erect, with a voice by no means indicating such a degree of physical weakness as did, in fact, possess him, with clear tones, and an impressive, and, I may say, an imposing manner, who did not feel that he might imagine that we saw before us a Senator of Rome, when Rome survived.

Sir, I have not in public nor in private life, known a more assiduous person in the discharge of his appropriate duties. I have known no man who wasted less of life in what is called recreation, or employed less of it in any pursuits not connected with the immediate discharge of his duty. He seemed to have no recreation but the pleasure of conversation with his friends. Out of the chambers of Congress, he

was either devoting himself to the acquisition of knowledge per-
taining to the immediate subject of the duty before him, or else
he was indulging in those social interviews in which he so much delighted. . . .

Mr. President, he had the basis, the indispensable basis, of all high
character; and that was, unspotted integrity—unimpeached honor and
character. If he had aspirations, they were high, and honorable, and
noble. There was nothing groveling, or low, or meanly selfish, that
came near the head or the heart of Mr. Calhoun. Firm in his purpose,
perfectly patriotic and honest, as I am sure he was, in the principles
that he espoused, and in the measures that he defended, aside from
that large regard for that species of distinction that conducted him to
eminent stations for the benefit of the republic, I do not believe he
had a selfish motive, or selfish feeling.

However, sir, he may have differed from others of us in his political
opinions, or his political principles, those principles and those
opinions will now descend to posterity under the sanction of a great
name. He has lived long enough, he has done enough, and he has
done it so well, so successfully, so honorably, as to connect himself
for all time with the records of his country. He is now an historical
character. Those of us who have known him here, will find that he
has left upon our minds and our hearts a strong and lasting impression of his person, his character, and his public performances, which,
while we live, will never be obliterated. We shall hereafter, I am sure,
indulge in it as a grateful recollection that we have lived in his age,
that we have been his contemporaries, that we have seen him, and
heard him, and known him. We shall delight to speak of him to those
who are rising up to fill our places. And, when the time shall come
when we ourselves shall go, one after another, in succession, to our
graves, we shall carry with us a deep sense of his genius and character, his honor and integrity, his amiable deportment in private
life, and the purity of his exalted patriotism.

FREDERICK DOUGLASS AND OTHERS: FRIENDS AND
ADVERSARIES, BLACK AND WHITE

*Calhoun's gift for winning over those opposed to him is a
matter of record; a man named William Smith complained that
Calhoun had treated him with such kindness, consideration, and*

courtesy that he "could not hate him as much as I wanted to do." George Washington Featherstonhaugh may have thought Calhoun the most perfect gentleman he had ever met, but historian James Parton declared that "his mind was as arrogant as his manners were courteous. Everyone who ever conversed with him must remember his positive, peremptory, unanswerable 'Not all all, not at all,' whenever one of his favorite positions was assailed." "I desire never to meet him again," one Charlestonian burst out. "I hate a man who makes me think so much."

One of the most scathing commentaries ever delivered on Calhoun was a private outburst by the eccentric Virginian, John Randolph of Roanoke, delivered in the wake of their bitter debate over the War of 1812. "You are wide of the mark," Randolph wrote his friend, J. M. Garnett, "when you suppose that my gentle correction of the Yale College orator has produced any sensible effect. That gentleman has not been educated in Connecticut for nothing. He unites to the savage ferocity of the frontierman all the insensibility of the Yankee character in a compound most marvelously offensive to every man having pretensions to the character of a gentleman." Randolph thought the South Carolinian to be over-bearing, insolent, and supercilious. "He has all the cold unfeeling Yankee manner with the bitter and acrimonious irritability of the South—at least of some Southern men whom I have known." [10]

For all his charm, Calhoun's intensity was tiring, if not tiresome, to those who knew him best. Alabama Congressman Dixon Lewis, Calhoun's close companion at one period, complained that he could find no repose in him, that whenever he sought relaxation, Calhoun would work him to a higher pitch, "in some kind of excitement." His devoted disciple and secretary, Richard Crallé, found him "too intelligent, too industrious, too intent on the struggle of politics to suit me except as an occasional companion."

Political associates felt the weight of his intensity and his humorlessness; "a humbug," Benton called him, and the Charlestonian Hugh Legaré described him as "a monomaniac consumed by a single idea." Henry Clay mocked him: "tall, careworn, with furrowed brow, haggard and intensely gazing, looking as if he

[10] John Randolph to J. M. Garnett, February 5, 1812. From "The Letterbook of John Randolph of Roanoke," Garnett Collection, University of Virginia Library. Used by permission of the University of Virginia Library.

were dissecting the last abstraction which sprung from the meta-physician's brain, and muttering to himself in half-uttered tones, 'This is indeed a crisis.'" Calhoun's lifelong political associate, James Hammond, even denied his gift for friendship. "Could he have conversed with every individual in the United States," Hammond wrote, "none could have stood against him"; yet added, bitterly, "He marches and countermarches all who follow him, until having broken from the bulk of his followers he breaks from his friends one by one and expends them in breaking down his late associates—so all ends in ruin." Many complained that he thought for the state, that he was like a great tree overshadowing South Carolina, choking out all expression and opposition to him.

William Lloyd Garrison's evaluation, written after Calhoun's famed fourth of March speech, was predictable; Calhoun "had no breadth of character, no greatness of spirit, no generosity of purpose, no comprehensiveness of view." A man should be known by his heart, rather than his brain, and Calhoun had no heart; "he was made of iron, not flesh." Upon Calhoun's death a few weeks later, he wrote, "His memory shall rot, or be remembered by future generations only to be execrated for his tyrannical and impious principles." Paradoxically, both Calhoun and Garrison saw that the Constitution was a compromise with slavery.

But the reaction of the great Negro leader and abolitionist, Frederick Douglass, was completely unpredictable. He discussed Calhoun frequently over the years: "this mighty man," he called him, "the master spirit of the South, the great champion of human bondage." Unlike Garrison, he saw Calhoun's last speech as "though exceedingly defective . . . creditable and praise-worthy. It is plain, straightforward, and consistent, and it shows that the object aimed for, infernal though it be, is devoutly wished for by its author." By diagnosing the disease, rather than prescribing a remedy, Douglass believed he offered proof that "the tyrant-power of Calhoun, in this nation, is broken; the great object of his life has been attacked by an overwhelming force; and he has no arm to defend it." Calhoun, not Seward, he saw as "the original author of the doctrine of the irrepressible conflict," and he was frank to concede Calhoun's clear logic, if you granted his premise: "The slaveholder has the best of the argument the very moment the legality and constitutionality of slavery is conceded."

But of what Calhoun called "the peculiar domestic institution," Douglass thundered:

Better call it *Domestic Robbery Institution.* To buy and sell, to brand and scourge human beings with the heavy lash—to rob them of all the just rewards of their labor—to compel them to live in ignorance of their relations to God and man—to blot out the institution of marriage—to herd men and women together like the beasts of the field—to deprive them of the means of learning to read the name of God—to destroy their dignity as human beings—to record their names on the ledger with horses, sheep, and swine—to feed them on a peck of corn a week—to work them under a burning sun in the rice swamp, cottonfield, sugar plantation, almost in a state of nudity —to sunder families for the convenience of purchasers—to examine men, women, and children, on the auction block, as a jockey would examine a horse—to punish them for a word, look, or gesture—to burn their flesh with hot irons—to tear their backs with the poisonous claws of a living cat—to shoot, stab, and hunt humanity with bloodhounds,—for one class of men to have exclusive and absolute power over the bodies and souls of another class of human beings; this, the whole of this infernal catalogue, is comprehended in the soft and innocent term, *"domestic institution."* This is the established order of things in Carolina; and Mr. Calhoun and his "forty thieves" would have the same order of things in California. But now to the doctrine laid down in the above extract.—It goes the length of denying, on *moral* grounds, to any and every person out of the State where slavery exists, the right of saying, looking, or doing anything, directly or indirectly, for the overthrow of slavery.—According to this reasoning, it would be immoral for Northern men to refuse to wear slave-grown cotton, or to eat slave-grown rice and sugar, since by pursuing such a course, peradventure they might decrease the value of the slaves, and thereby indirectly affect the permanence of slavery. We are not to write, speak, or publish anything on the subject of human slavery, lest it serve to darken the fame of slavery, and lessen it in the popular estimation, and thereby indirectly destroy slavery, by exalting liberty. To do so, would necessarily be a flagrant aggression, a violation of the rights of a State, and subversive of its government. For what we have no right to do directly by legislation, we have no right to do indirectly by any other means.—This is strange logic for one of the most powerful minds and renowned statesmen that America affords. Coming from another quarter, it would demand no answer or comment; but from such a man, endorsed by such a company, read so universally, and put forth so imposingly, and solemnly, aiming as it does, at the very foundation of the antislavery movement, it may be proper to spend a few thoughts upon it.

How completely has slavery triumphed over the mind of this strong man! It holds full, complete, and absolute control in his mind; so much so, that seeing it, he cannot and does not desire to see anything else than slavery. The right of speech, the freedom of the press, the liberty of assembling, and the right of petition, have in his judgment no rightful existence in the Constitution of the United States.

Slavery is there; he knows it to be there; it has a right to be there; and anything inconsistent with it is wrong, immoral, and has no right to be there. This is evidently the state of mind which Mr. Calhoun brings to the consideration of this subject. To reduce his reasoning to its real point and pith, it amounts to this—that where a people have no power to legislate for the overthrow of what *they think* an evil, they have no moral right to think, or speak, or do anything else which may induce those who have legislative power to exercise it for the removal of such evil. It is on this reasoning that he builds his complaint against the Northern states, as wanting in respect to the institutions and sovereignty of the Southern states; that they have not by legislative enactment silenced the voice of free speech, and suppressed the publications of the abolitionists. If Mr. Calhoun is right in his first position, he is right in his conclusion; but he is wrong in both. We have no legislative power to dethrone the Queen of England, but have we no moral right to say that England would be better under a republican form of government? We have no legislative right or power to alter or abolish the British tariff; but have we no moral right to say that it is unequal and oppressive, and that England would be better off without than with it. We have no legislative power to abolish the union between England and Ireland; yet is it not obviously our right to speak and write in favor of the repeal of the Union? Mr. Calhoun sinks the rights of the man in the duties of the citizen, and by confounding things which are separate and distinct, perpetrates a logical fallacy. Above and before all human institutions, stands the right of sympathizing with the oppressed and denouncing the oppressors of mankind.

Slavery is not only a wrong done to the slave, but an outrage upon man—not merely a curse to the South, but to the whole Union, and has no rightful existence anywhere.—Slaveholders have no rights.

* * *

Mr. Calhoun and his "forty thieves" see and clearly comprehend the moral forces now operating against slavery, and is too honest towards his fellow companions in crime to conceal the danger which besets, or to affect to despise that danger. He is proud, haughty, and bitter, but not defiant. He sees in the systematic agitation—the tracts, pictures, papers, pamphlets, and books—societies, lectures, and petitions, the most efficient means to bring about a state of things which will force the South into emancipation.[11]

* * *

Selfishness . . . has at length ultimated into the formation of a party, ranged under the very taking appellation of National—the greatest business of which is to hold at bay, and restrain, and if possible to extinguish in the heart of this great nation every sentiment supposed to be at variance with the safety of slavery.

This party has arisen out of the teachings of that great man of perverted faculties, the late John C. Calhoun. No man of the nation has left a broader or a blacker mark on the politics of the nation, than he. In the eye of Mr. Calhoun every right guaranteed by the American Constitution, must be held in subordination to slavery. It was he who first boldly declared the self-evident truths of the declaration of independence, self-evident falsehoods. He has been followed in this by Mr. Benton D. D. from Indiana.

The very spirit of Mr. Calhoun animates the slavery party of today. His principles are its principles, and his philosophy its philosophy. He looked upon slavery as the great American interest. The slavery party of today so esteem it. To preserve it, shield it, and support it, is its constant duty, and the object and aim of all its exertions. With this party the right of free men, free labor, and a free north are nothing. Daniel Webster never said a truer word than at Marshfield, in '48— "Why the North? There is no North!" But there is a South and ever has been a South controlling both parties, at every period of their existence.

* * *

One other word for my subject. A grand movement on the part of mankind, in any direction, or for any purpose, moral or political, is an interesting fact, fit and proper to be studied. It is such, not only for those who eagerly participate in it, but also for those who stand

[11] From *The North Star*, Vol. I (February 9, 1849).

aloof from it—even for those by whom it is opposed. I take the anti-slavery movement to be such an one, and a movement as sublime and glorious, in its character, as it is holy and beneficent in the ends it aims to accomplish. At this moment, I deem it safe to say, it is properly engrossing more minds in this country than any other subject now before the American people. The late John C. Calhoun—one of the mightiest men that ever stood up in the American Senate—did not deem it beneath him; and he probably studied it as deeply, though not as honestly, as Gerrit Smith, or William Lloyd Garrison. He evinced the greatest familiarity with the subject; and the greatest efforts of his last years in the Senate had direct reference to this movement. His eagle eye watched every new development connected with it; and he was ever prompt to inform the South of every important step in its progress. He never allowed himself to make light of it; but always spoke of it and treated it as a matter of grave import; and, in this, he showed himself a master of the mental, moral, and religious constitution of human society. Daniel Webster, too, in the better days of his life, before he gave his assent to the Fugitive Slave Bill, and trampled upon all his earlier and better convictions—when his eye was yet single—he clearly comprehended the nature of the elements involved in this movement; and in his own majestic eloquence, warned the South, and the country, to have a care how they attempted to put it down. He is an illustration that it is easier to give, than to take good advice. To these two men—the greatest men to whom the nation has yet given birth—may be traced the two great facts of the present—the South triumphant, and the North humbled. Their names may stand thus: Calhoun and domination—Webster and degradation.[12]

[12] From Frederick Douglass Paper, Vol. II (November 24, 1854).

10
Calhoun in Retrospect

Calhoun has suffered the unique fate of being the ac-
knowledged leader of a cause fought and lost years after his own
death. Retrospective judgments were therefore highly prejudiced.
Looking back on Calhoun's words as spoken over fifty years before,
Massachusetts Yankee Josiah Quincy read into them nuances
foreshadowing the great conflict of the 60s. Even the sympathetic
Walter Miller, writing in the Albany Law Journal *at the turn of*
the century acknowledged that "Calhoun believed slavery was
right and millions of the best people the sun ever shone on
agreed with him," but added that "there seemed to be a tinge of
sadness pervading Mr. Calhoun during all the latter years of his
life. He was fighting against fate and he seemed at times almost
to realize it. His speeches . . . had about them . . . the pro-
phetic warnings of a seer. . . . There was something pathetic in
his appearance in the Senate on the occasion of his last great
speech . . . with the weight of years and illness upon him." [1]
His "great error," Miller thought, was in his failure to see that
the whole world was against slavery, and that some plan of
gradual emancipation should have been worked out. Few at this
period would have agreed with the English historian Percy
Gregg, who flatly declared Calhoun to be "after Alexander
Hamilton, the most consistent, logical, clear-sighted, and far-
sighted statesman, the profoundest thinker that the Union has
ever produced, the greatest, ablest, most resolute of that third
political generation, who were fated to wrestle with the threat of
a dividing Union." To many Calhoun seemed the evil genius of
the conflict, or, as Ben Perley Poore, clerk of the House of Repre-
sentatives, put it—"the arch-traitor like Satan in Paradise." Many
saw the dividing Union and the Civil War as the fruition of the
plotting of John C. Calhoun.

[1] *The Albany Law Journal* (January 7, 1899), pp. 17–34.

WILLIAM H. CHANNING: "THE GRAND-MASTER OF THE CONSPIRATORS" [2]

The origin of this strife is *a conspiracy of the Slave Oligarchy, to ruin, because they can no longer rule, the Republic of the United States.* By Conspiracy is meant a plot of treason. The conspirators are the Slave Oligarchy, for the germ of this plot is a purpose to perpetuate and extend the Slave System; and the ringleaders of the conspiracy are a *few* ambitious and designing men. Trained and habituated to sway the policy of the United States, they cannot consent to drop the sceptre, they have so long wielded. . . .

The home and hiding place of this conspiracy for long years was South Carolina: and the Grand-Master of the conspirators was the late John C. Calhoun. Mr. Calhoun was a man of sagacity and forecast, of stern logic and indomitable will; he wore an air of great personal dignity; and as a citizen, neighbour, and friend was everywhere spoken of with admiring respect. But he was also a man of soaring ambition, that knew no bounds; and his dauntless self-confidence brooked no superior. He was professionally a politician, and from early life he planned to manage the Democratic party, so as to serve the exclusive ends of the Slave-power.

* * *

Hence, then, the earnestness with which a few leaders of the Slave Oligarchy insisted upon the doctrine of "State Rights," in preparation for the inevitable period of Dissolution. The *pretext* for the "Nullification" movement, in 1832–33, was the emancipation of South Carolina from the burden of an obnoxious tariff; but the latent *purpose* of Nullification was to train the conscience and mind of the people of that State, and of all the Southern States, to the assertion of the sovereign rights of each separate State. In Nullification, Mr. Calhoun craftily planted the germ of Secession. Nullification was the exercise of the State Rights *within* the Union, the roots striking down to weaken and undermine the stately structure; Secession is the exercise of State Rights to dissolve the Union, the giant parasite subverting in ruins the commonwealth. Finding that he could not unite the South for disunion upon the tariff question, as Louisiana would have a tariff upon sugar, Mr. Calhoun declared to his followers, "we must force an

[2] From William Henry Channing, *The Civil War in America*, pamphlet (Liverpool, 1861), pp. 7, 10.

issue on the Slavery question." Andrew Jackson, when President of the United States in 1833, was speaking from thorough knowledge of the plot and the plotters, when he wrote:—"Take care of your Nullifiers: you have them among you. Let them meet with the indignant frowns of every man who loves his country. The tariff, it is now known, was a mere pretext, . . . and *Disunion* and a *Southern Confederacy* were the real object. The next pretext will be the *Negro or Slavery question*."

The poison plant was a generation in growing, which has borne the bitter fruit of secession. . . .

HERMANN VON HOLST: "THE GREATEST AND PUREST OF PRO-SLAVERY FANATICS" [3]

As yet it is hardly possible to pass an unbiased judgment upon him, because the wounds of the terrible conflict, in which he was during the lifetime of a whole generation the acknowledged leader, have not fully healed, and therefore those passions have not completely died away which were engendered by the catastrophe in which that conflict ended. Meanwhile, it becomes every day more difficult really to understand that struggle. . . . There is no other instance in all the history of the the world where the civilizations of two different ages, with their antagonistic principles and modes of thinking and feeling, have been as intricately interwoven as in the United States during the times of the slavery conflict. It is only the part played by Calhoun in this conflict which puts him into the very first rank of the men who have acted on the political stage of the United States, though he has done enough else to secure for his name a permanent place in the annals of his country.

As the years roll on, the fame of Daniel Webster and Henry Clay is gradually growing dimmer, while the name of Calhoun has yet lost hardly anything of the lurid intensity with which it glowed on the political firmament of the United States towards the end of the first half of this century. Nor will it ever lose much of this.

*　　*　　*

To the last moment, he manifested the deepest interest and concern in the troubles of his country. "The South! The poor South!

[3] From Hermann von Holst, *John C. Calhoun* (Boston, 1882), pp. 2–4, 349–51.

God knows what will become of her!" murmured his trembling lips,
but he died with that serenity of mind which only a clear conscience
can give on the deathbed. On February 12, 1847, he had said in the
Senate, "If I know myself, if my head was at stake, I would do my
duty, be the consequences what they might." It was his solemn conviction that throughout his life he had faithfully done his duty, both
to the Union and to his section, because, as he honestly believed
slavery to be "a good, a positive good," he had never been able to see
that it was impossible to serve at the same time the Union and his
section, if his section was considered as identical with the slavocracy.
In perfect faith he had undertaken what no man could accomplish,
because it was a physical and moral impossibility: antagonistic principles cannot be united into a basis on which to rest a huge political
fabric. Nullification and the government of law; state supremacy and
a constitutional Union, endowed with the power necessary to minister
to the wants of a great people; the nationalization of slavery upon the
basis of states-rightism in a federal Union, composed principally of
free communities, by which slavery was considered a sin and a curse;
equality of States and constitutional consolidation of geographical
sections, with an artificial preponderance granted to the minority,—
these were incompatibilities, and no logical ingenuity could reason
them together into the formative principle of a gigantic commonwealth. The speculations of the keenest political logician the United
States had ever had ended in the greatest logical monstrosity imagina-
ble, because his reasoning started from a *contradictio in adjecto*. This
he failed to see, because the mad delusion had wholly taken possession
of his mind that in this age of steam and electricity, of democratic
ideas and the rights of man, slavery was "the most solid foundation
of liberty." More than to any other man, the South owed it to him that
she succeeded for such a long time in forcing the most democratic
and the most progressive commonwealth of the universe to bend its
knees and do homage to the idol of this "peculiar institution"; but
therefore also the largest share of the responsibility for what at last
did come rests on his shoulders.

No man can write the last chapter of his own biography, in which
the *Facit* of his whole life is summed up, so to say, in one word. If
ever a new edition of the works of the greatest and purest of proslavery fanatics should be published, it ought to have a short appendix
—the emancipation proclamation of Abraham Lincoln.

JAMES PARTON: "HIS ATTACHMENT TO THE UNION WAS CONDITIONAL AND SUBORDINATE" [4]

From the beginning of his public career there was a canker in he heart of it; for, while his oath, as a member of Congress, to sup-port the Constitution of the United States, was still fresh upon his lips, he declared that his attachment to the Union was conditional and subordinate. He said that the alliance between the Southern planters nd Northern Democrats was a false and calculated compact, to be broken when the planters could no longer rule by it. While he resided n Washington, and acted with the Republican party in the flush of ts double triumph, he appeared a respectable character, and won olden opinions from eminent men in both parties. But when he was gain subjected to the narrowing and perverting influence of a res-dence in South Carolina, he shrunk at once to his original propor-ions, and became thenceforth, not the servant of his country, but the pecial pleader of a class and the representative of a section. And yet, with that strange judicial blindness which has ever been the doom of he defenders of wrong, he still hoped to attain the Presidency. There s scarcely any example of infatuation more remarkable than this. Here we have, lying before us at this moment, undeniable proofs, in he form of "campaign lives" and "campaign documents," that, as ate as 1844 there was money spent and labor done for the purpose of placing him in nomination for the highest office.

Calhoun failed in all the leading objects of his public life, except one; but in that one his success will be memorable forever. He has eft it on record (see [Thomas Hart] Benton [*Thirty Years' View*], II, 98) that his great aim, from 1835 to 1847, was to force the slavery ssue on the North. "It is our duty," he wrote in 1847, "to force the ssue on the North." "Had the South," he continued, "or even my own tate, backed me, I would have forced the issue on the North in 835"; and he welcomed the Wilmot Proviso in 1847 because, as he privately wrote, it would be the means of "enabling us to force the ssue on the North." In this design, at length, when he had been ten ears in the grave, he succeeded. Had there been no Calhoun, it is possible—nay, it is not improbable—that that issue might have been

[4] From James Parton, *Famous Americans of Recent Times* (Boston, 1874), pp. 28–29, 142–43, 156–57, 170–71.

deferred till the North had so outstripped the South in accumulating all the elements of power, that the fire-eaters themselves would have shrunk from submitting the question to the arbitrament of the sword. It was Calhoun who forced the issue upon the United States, and compelled us to choose between annihilation and war.

PART THREE

JOHN C. CALHOUN
IN HISTORY

With the romanticizing of the lost cause at the end of the nineteenth century, the tides of historical opinion began to flow in Calhoun's direction. The forerunner of the new trend was Jabez L. M. Curry, who stated: "He was preeminently, almost idolatrously, a friend of the Union . . . of coequal states." Curry wrote that "no one was readier to make sacrifices for the Union, whose element was the Constitution. . . . Entering public life in early manhood, the one pole star by which his path was guided . . . was the honor of the whole country." [1] Generally sympathetic studies were written by Gaillard Hunt and William E. Dodd, among others, and in 1917 appeared the first full-length biography of Calhoun, an objective but uninspiring account by William Meigs.

A landmark in Calhoun historiography was Vernon Parrington's essay, "John C. Calhoun, Realist," in his monumental Main Currents of American Thought. *For the first time a major scholar contended that Calhoun's political philosophy, in particular his idea of proportional representation, had validity beyond its own time, and within the framework of the American political system. "Commanding every highway of the Southern mind," Parrington wrote, "Calhoun recast the philosophy of the fathers —dissected the weaknesses of popular democracy, and erected a last barrier against consolidation and standardization which was 'blown to pieces by the guns of the Civil War.'" Parrington saw Calhoun as far more than the doomed symbol of slavery and the lost cause. So too did the British historian Christopher Hollis, who described Calhoun as "the personification of an idea," the symbol of a Southern civilization which, though based on slavery, stood as the last barrier to the triumph of industrial capitalism and the wage-slavery that industrialism brings.*

In 1937 Charles M. Wiltse expanded Parrington's concept of

---

[1] Jabez L. M. Curry, *Principles, Acts and Utterances of John C. Calhoun, Promotive of the True Union of the States* (Chicago, 1898), p. 11.

Calhoun's doctrine of the concurrent majority. His subsequen three-volume biography is the most exhaustive and thoroug study yet undertaken of Calhoun and his ideas.

Richard Current saw the key to Calhoun's political philosoph as the class struggle; this idea was expanded a few years later b Richard Hofstadter, in his essay, "John C. Calhoun: The Kar Marx of the Master Class." Hofstadter dismissed Calhoun's ide of the concurrent majority as having no interest for the twen tieth-century mind, but saw his scheme of social analysis a "worthy of considerable respect." Economist Peter Drucker, o the other hand, saw in Calhoun's concept of sectional and in terest pluralism the key to the understanding of the America political system. In this tradition, I contended that Calhoun, i practice, if not in theory, repudiated states' rights completely a a workable mechanism by 1850. I also contended that it is a mis conception to depict him as Wiltse did, as having changed from a nationalist to a sectionalist, but that he had been both con currently throughout his entire career.²

Louis Hartz, in an essay, "South Carolina Versus the Unite States," dissected the fallacies in the nullification argumen pointing out that Calhoun had substituted legalisms for th spirit of compromise which alone would make the legalisms wor Calhoun had dealt with the deepest issues that confront societ and had striven unsuccessfully to superimpose law upon th very chaos that would inevitably destroy society. New insight into the nullification doctrine have been supplied by the writing of William Freehling.

²Margaret L. Coit, "Calhoun and the Downfall of States' Rights," *Virgini Quarterly Review*, XXVIII (Spring, 1952), 191–208.

11

William E. Dodd: "Calhoun was a Nationalist in His Heart to the Day of His Death"[1]

Not many of us know John C. Calhoun as he was, as he lived and moved among Americans of the last century. No political party looks back to Calhoun as its founder or rejuvenator, no group of public men proclaim allegiance to his doctrines, no considerable group of individuals outside of South Carolina profess any love for his name and ideals. While all parties seek to find in Jefferson's writings justification for their programs, one dare admit their present policy to be even remotely descended from the teaching of the great Carolinian; yet Calhoun had the approval while a young man of the great Virginian and died more beloved by a greater number of Americans than even the Sage of Monticello. When Jefferson died Virginia wept, but not loudly; when Calhoun's body was carried to Charleston in April, 1850, the whole state mourned as though each man had lost his father. For weeks the ordinary course of business was interrupted and months afterward men talked gloomily as they met upon the streets of Charleston. Only twice in the history of the country have men felt so keenly the loss of one of their leaders—December, 1799, and April, 1864.

It was a simple life that Calhoun led, yet tragedy played with him as with its true child, and a tragic fate awaited in 1850 those who saw the grave close over his mortal remains; and today the people of a great state think of him as of no other American and linger sadly about the tomb where their fathers laid him—a people who still feel more keenly than all others the weight of Sherman's terrible blows in 1864 and 1865, who still insist that their cause and his was just.

* * *

Calhoun held impetuous South Carolina in tow from 1828 to 1832, and this was a feat which not only showed the great power of the man

[1] From William E. Dodd, *Statesmen of the Old South* (New York, 1911), pp. 91–92, 117–18, 133–35, 166–67. Copyright 1911 by The Macmillan Company; renewed 1967, copyright holder unknown. If there is a known address for the executors of the estate of William E. Dodd, please notify Prentice-Hall, Inc., Englewood Cliffs, New Jersey.

but his love for the nation. What he hoped to do was to brin Congress to a reasonable tariff, say a general average of 20%, wit which all the South would have been pleased and which would hav been ample protection to Northern manufacturers, and then, attainin the leadership of the country, go on with the great nationalizing wor of knitting the South and West together. And in view of what th tariff has done for us and of Calhoun's unequaled influence and powe as shown in after years, who will say this was not the correct course It had been the union of the South and West which sustained Jeffe son's administrations; cooperation of South and West was still th basis of the national policy; and there are those among us today wh look for a solution of our twentieth-century troubles only from friendly understanding between these really democratic sections c the country. . . .

. . . It has been customary in American history writing to treat Ca houn from 1833 to his death in 1850, as an archconspirator, seekin the overthrow of the government which he served and upon which h had bestowed the best years of his life. I am constrained to view hi differently. Calhoun was a nationalist at heart to the day of his deat and in the intimacy of private correspondence he spoke of a severe nation "bleeding at every pore"—a state of things which he said h could not think of encouraging. What he was striving for during th last seventeen years of his life was the building of a "solid" Sout which should follow his teaching implicitly and which, cast into th scales of national politics, would decide all great questions in its favo And it cannot be doubted that he expected to be elevated to th Presidency as a natural result—a position which he coveted as warml as did Henry Clay himself. It was not his aim to break up the Unio but to dominate it.

His method of uniting the people of the South was to show ther that without such union the greatest interest of their section, slavery was doomed. Calhoun sought to weld together his people on a basi of economic interest just as Clay had sought to build a "solid" Nort on the basis of a high tariff. On this subject parties had ceased t differ in large sections of the North. Rhode Island Democrats wer "tariff" Democrats; Pennsylvania made protection *a sine qua non* o cooperation with the party of Jackson; Kentucky, Ohio, and the North west voted solidly for that policy of the nation which was thought t operate in their favor. The South, regardless of party lines, ha come to regard slavery as either a good thing or an evil which coul not, and ought not, to be eradicated; Whigs vied with Democrats i asseverating their loyalty to the "peculiar institution." Slavery wa uglier in outward appearance than protection, but in principle Negro servitude and a protective tariff were alike—each meant the exploitation of the weaker and more ignorant classes of society by the wealthier and more intelligent. As a matter of morals there was no difference between the demand of the Western Reserve that a prohibitive tariff in favor of their wool be maintained by the federal government and that of South Carolina that Negro slavery should be forever guaranteed. A high tariff on wool compelled the poor white man to give his labor to others without recompense; slavery compelled the Negro to work for his master without reward.

* * *

No man doubts what Calhoun stood for; and the people of the South know well that it was he who prepared the way for secession and war. The author has heard small cotton farmers declaim how the South would have won but for his death ten years before the war.

He had begun, the son of a small planter, whose father had been an antislavery man, had become a slave-holder through no fault of his own, married a lady of the aristocratic regime in Charleston, and turned his attention to national politics. He became at once an ardent nationalist, impelled onward by the sectionalism of New England, and was one of the great figures of that period of reconstruction which followed the second war with England. Compelled by the injustice and bad faith of a personal and despotic party leader, he turned his matchless genius to the invention of a doctrine which should reconcile nationality with particularism, and became at once the champion of slavery and cotton, the money interests of the South. From 1833 to 1850 he taught the South that property in Negro slaves was more sacred than the rights and ideas so eloquently defended, by his own great teacher, Jefferson. He died, the greatest reactionary of his time.

War was to be the next stage in the evolution, and Jefferson Davis was to complete the work of Calhoun and convert the old and radical democracy of Jefferson into armies contending upon the field of battle for ideals and purposes absolutely foreign to the mind of the great founder.

12

Vernon L. Parrington: "The Master Political Mind of the South"[1]

The greatest figure in that long controversy was certainly John C. Calhoun, a man who set his face like flint against every northern middle-class ambition, and with his dream of a Greek democracy steered his beloved South upon the rocks. A truly notable figure was this ascetic Carolinian. In the passionate debates over slavery he daily matched powers with Webster and Clay and proved himself intellectually the greatest of the three. He is the one outstanding political thinker in a period singularly barren and uncreative. His influence was commanding. Tall, lean, eager, with no humor, no playfulness, lacking the magnetic personality of Clay and the ornate rhetoric of Webster, speaking plainly and following his logic tenaciously, this gaunt Scotch-Irishman became by virtue of intellect and character, driven by an apostolic zeal, the master political mind of the South, an uncrowned king who carried his native Carolina in his pocket like a rotten borough. Long before his death he had expanded a political philosophy into a school of thought. What he planned a hundred disciples hastened to execute. Like Jefferson he was a pervasive influence in shaping men's opinions. It was impossible to ignore him or to escape the admonitory finger that pointed at every weak and shuffling compromiser.

Whatever road one travels one comes at last upon the austere figure of Caulhoun, commanding every highway of the southern mind. He subjected the philosophy of the fathers to critical analysis; pointed out wherein he conceived it to be faulty; cast aside some of its most sacred doctrines; provided another foundation for the democratic faith which he professed. And when he had finished the great work of reconstruction, the old Jeffersonianism that had satisfied the mind of Virginia was reduced to a thing of shreds and patches, acknowl-

[1] From Vernon L. Parrington, *The Romantic Revolution in America* (New York, 1927), pp. 69–70, 72–74, 75–78, 81–82.

edged by his followers to have been a mistaken philosophy, blinded by romantic idealism and led astray by French humanitarianism. To substitute realism for idealism, to set class economics above abstract humanitarianism, was the mission to which Calhoun devoted himself. He undid for the plantation South the work of his old master. Speaking in the name of democracy, he attacked the foundations on which the democratic movement in America had rested, substituting for its libertarian and equalitarian doctrines conceptions wholly alien and antagonistic to western democracy, wholly Greek in their underlying spirit.

Calhoun's career was linked indissolubly with slavery. He was the advocate and philosopher of southern imperialism, and in defense of that imperialism he elaborated those particularist theories which prepared the way for the movement of secession.

* * *

Calhoun's contribution to political theory—a contribution that elevates him to a distinguished place among American political thinkers—was the child of necessity, and received its particularist bias from the exigencies of sectional partisanship. With the rapid expansion of the nation westward, and the consequent augmenting of a potentially hostile free-soil power, the South was doomed to become increasingly a minority voice in the councils of government; and if it were to preserve its peculiar institution it must find more adequate means of self-protection than it had enjoyed hitherto. The tendencies most to be feared, in his judgment, were the spontaneous drift towards consolidation, and an uncritical faith in numerical majorities. He was convinced that America had too thoughtlessly accepted the principle of political democracy as a sufficient safeguard against the danger of arbitrary government. Soon or late it must discover, what the South already was discovering, that numerical democracy, unrestrained by constitutional limitations on its will, is no friend to political justice. The critical test of every government is the measure of protection afforded its weakest citizen; and judged by this test a democratic state, when power has come to be centralized in few hands, may prove to be no other than a tyrant. Irresponsible in its unrestraint, the majority vote may easily outdo an Oriental despot in arbitrary rule, and the more power it wields the more ruthless will be its disregard of minority opinion. The political philosopher who proposes to formulate an ideal democratic system of government, therefore, must deal critically with this fundamental problem of political justice, for upon the solution will turn the excellence and permanence of every democracy. It was to this baffling problem that Calhoun addressed himself.

In seeking a constitutional defense for the threatened southern interests, he drew from the two great reservoirs of American constitutional theory. From the Jeffersonian Republicans he derived his familiar doctrine of states' rights in opposition to the consolidating principle; from the Federalists of the Montesquieu school he drew his theory of static government, resulting from exactly balanced powers; and from the amalgamation of these diverse theories he formulated a new principle. Both schools of earlier thought, he had come to believe, had been sound in their major premises, but both had gone astray in certain important deductions. The experience of forty years, with the democracy constantly augmenting its powers, had demonstrated to Calhoun's satisfaction both the grave danger that lay in the principle of consolidation, and the insufficiency of existing checks on the federal government. The prime mistake of the Jeffersonians, he conceived, was their belief that the democratic majority will necessarily serve the cause of political justice; and the miscalculation of the Federalists resulted from the belief that the division of powers provided in the Constitution was adequate to prevent arbitrary government. He now proposed to correct these two mistakes by providing an additional check through the simple expedient—as logical as it was efficacious, granted his premises—of recognizing the veto power of the individual commonwealth upon an act of the federal government. Stripped of its states'-rights limitation, this was in germ the principle of the referendum, modified, however, by certain suggestive provisions.

The veto power as a protective principle Calhoun regarded as the hallmark of constitutional government. Granted that sovereignty under the Constitution inheres in the people, and that all authority is delegated, it follows that government is no more than an agent with strictly defined fiduciary powers, all the acts of which are subject to review by the principal. Whether such review shall be immediate and plenary, or at more or less remote and limited, becomes therefore a fundamental question of constitutional polity. Unfortunately much confusion has resulted from an intentional vagueness, contributed by interested groups to further particular ends, in the common understanding of the terms, the people and government. The former is rarely, as is usually assumed, a homogeneous body with common interests, but a congeries of individuals and groups and classes with diverse and often antagonistic interests; and the latter—in a republic —is never a sacred entity, the residuary legatee of sovereignty, to criticize which is to commit the crime of *lèse majesté*, but a group of officials invested with temporary authority and actuated by motives common to all men.

*   *   *

Every realist knows that "the people" is a political fiction. Society is made up of individuals, each with his particular interest. The total interests of the subject-citizens are necessarily complex. Group and classify them as he may, the political philosopher can never merge the parts in a coalescing whole, but must recognize that the problem remains one of adjustments and compromises. It follows therefore that any facile assumption that government represents the people or rests on the will of the people is a disastrous fallacy. Popular government rests on the will of the majority; aristocratic government rests on the will of the aristocracy; and despotic government rests on the will of the despot. It is an axiom that the political state is partisan to those who administer it. The stakes of rulership are high; the game of politics never lacks its devotees; the business of deceiving the people in order to pluck the goose has long been one of the respectable professions.

The perennial problem of constitutional government, then, in Calhoun's philosophy, remains what it was seen to be by the Federalist followers of Montesquieu—the problem of restraining government by constitutional checks to the end that it be kept just. Existing machinery having demonstrated its inadequacy, it remained to provide more effective. Freedom Calhoun regarded as the crown jewel of civilization, hardly won, easily lost. But freedom was not to be measured by *habeas corpus* acts and similar legal restraints on tyranny; it was freedom from legal exploitation and statutory dictatorship. "The abuse of delegated power, and the tyranny of the stronger over the weaker interests, are the two dangers, and the only two to be guarded against; and if this be done effectually, liberty must be eternal. Of the two, the latter is the greater and most difficult to resist" (*Works,* Vol. VI, p. 32). In more definite terms the problem is thus stated:

> Two powers are necessary to the existence and preservation of free States: a power on the part of the ruled to prevent rulers from abusing their authority, by compelling them to be faithful to their constituents, and which is effected through the right of suffrage; and a power to compel the parts of society to be just to one another; by compelling them to consult the interest of each other—which can only be effected . . . by requiring the concurring assent of all the great and distinct interests of the community to the measures of the Government. This result is the sum-total of all the contrivances adopted by free States to

preserve their liberty, by preventing the conflicts between the sever;
classes or parts of the community. (*Ibid.,* Vol. VI, pp. 189–90.)

In elaboration of the second phase of the problem, Calhoun co*
tributed the principle on which his reputation as a political thinke
must rest—the doctrine of a concurrent majority. He found his solu
tion in an expansion of the principle of democracy—recovering th
true principle, he was fond of insisting—by superimposing upon th
consolidated, indiscriminate numerical majority the will of a gec
graphical majority; or in other words, by a special form of section*
referendum.

> It results, from what has been said, that there are two different mode
> in which the sense of the community may be taken: one, simply, by th
> right of suffrage, unaided; the other, by the right through a prope
> organism. Each collects the sense of the majority. But one regard
> numbers only, and considers the whole community one unit, havin
> but one common interest throughout; and collects the sense of th
> greater number of the whole, as that of the community. The other, o*
> the contrary, regards interests as well as numbers;—considering th*
> community as made up of different and conflicting interests as far a
> the action of the government is concerned; and takes the sense of each
> through its majority or appropriate organ, and the united sense o
> all, as the sense of the entire community. The former of these I cal
> the numerical, or absolute majority; and the latter, the concurrent, o
> constitutional majority. (*A Disquisition on Government,* in *Work*
> Vol. I, p. 28.)

In such speculation on the possibility of achieving political justic*
by the machinery of representation, Calhoun was face to face with ;
revolutionary conception—the conception of proportional economi*
representation. The idea was implicit in his assumption of an existin;
economic sectionalism that must find adequate expression throug!
political agencies. He had come to understand the futility of a miscel
laneous numerical majority; he had only to go back to eighteenth
century philosophy and substitute economic classes for economic sec
tionalism, finding his social cleavages in economic groups instead o*
geographical divisions, to have recast the whole theory of representa*
tion. Clearly, he had made enormous strides in his thinking. He hac
long since put behind him the philosophy of Jefferson. He had sub
jected the principle of democracy to critical scrutiny. But instead o
rejecting it as an unworkable hypothesis, as the Hamiltonian Federal
ists had done, he proposed to establish it on a sound and permanen
basis. The ideal of democracy he conceived to be the noblest in th*

whole field of political thought, but misunderstood and misapplied as it had been in America, it had become the mother of every mischief. This betrayal of democracy he laid at the door of the Jeffersonians. They had accepted too carelessly the romantic dogmas of the French school, and had come to believe that democracy was synonymous with political equalitarianism.

It was this false notion that had debased the noble ideal, and delivered it over to the hands of the mob. To assert that men are created free and equal is to fly in the face of every biological and social fact. The first business of the true democrat, therefore, was to reexamine the nature of democracy and strip away the false assumptions and vicious conclusions that had done it incalculable injury. The Greeks, he pointed out, understood its essential nature better than the moderns. Democracy assumes a copartnership among equals. Its only rational foundation is good will, and it can function only through compromise. From this it follows that in a society composed of high and low, capable and weak, worthy and unworthy—as every historical society has been composed—a universal democracy is impractical. The numerous body of social incompetents will suffer one of two fates: they will be exploited by the capable minority under the guise of free labor, or they will be accepted as the wards of society and protected by the free citizens—they must inevitably become either wage-slaves or bond-slaves, in either case incapable of maintaining the rights of free members of the commonwealth. Democracy is possible only in a society that recognizes inequality as a law of nature, but in which the virtuous and capable enter into a voluntary copartnership for the common good, accepting wardship of the incompetent in the interest of society. This was the Greek ideal and this ideal had created Greek civilization. . . .

. . . Thus in the end the political philosopher turns partisan to a cause. His fruitful speculations on the theory of representation, his inquiry into the economic basis of politics, remained incomplete, the larger reaches only half explored. Espousing the ideal of democracy, he yielded to the seductions of a Greek republic. . . . It was a curious dream, yet no more curious than his faith in an obsolete article in the Constitution to withstand the advance of a hostile economy. There is something almost tragic in the self-deception of this clear-minded realist in his appeal to a paper defense against economic forces. . . .

Lost faiths and repudiated prophets go down to a common grave. The living have little inclination to learn from the dead. The political principles of Calhoun have had scant justice done them by later generations who incline to accept the easy opinion that the cause which triumphs is altogether the better cause. What Calhoun so greatly feared has since come about. He erected a last barrier against the progress of middle-class ideals—consolidation in politics and standardization in society; against a universal cash-register evaluation of life: and the barrier was blown to pieces by the guns of the Civil War Historically he was the last spokesman of the great school of the eighteenth century.

13

Christopher Hollis: "The Personification of an Idea"[1]

To many it may seem surprising that, in a select quartet of American statesmen, the fourth place should be given to Calhoun. Americans are not wont to waste their time upon failures, nor Englishmen upon people of whom they have never heard. Yet the selection is, I think, just. Calhoun was, more than any other, the personification of an idea. Although that idea was defeated and destroyed, yet, if only that we may understand the history of the victors, it is necessary to understand the philosophy of the vanquished and to study the life of their leaders.

*　　*　　*

The South had only accepted the bargain of the Union on the assumption that the power of government would remain in the hands of the landed classes, who alone have that understanding of tradition without which no society can be healthy, and, finding that power was passing into the hands not only of the North but of the industrial North, she became more and more doubtful of the advantages of the bargain.

*　　*　　*

He did, it is true, see nothing morally wrong in slavery. Yet not through any love of slavery did he now throw himself passionately into this—his greatest—fight. What he objected to, was not the abolition of slavery, but abolition, brought about in such a way, imposed by the North upon the South. Such an abolition, he saw, must mean the ruin of white prestige and consequently of all Southern life. Nor did he throw himself into the defense of slavery because it was the easiest to defend of the Southern institutions, but, like a good strategist,

[1] From Christopher Hollis, *The American Heresy* (New York, 1930), pp. 82–83, 98, 110–11, 114–16, 121, 136–39, 143–45.

119

because it was the hardest. The South, he had now come to see, was faced with a hostile population, unable to understand the virtue of her civilization. She could therefore only hope to preserve her civilization by preserving complete autonomy. Once she allowed any institution to be subverted by external pressure, all her institutions were doomed.

* * *

If we admit his purpose, Calhoun was right to go out and meet every attack upon slavery. To allow it to be spoken of as a thing only to be tolerated was the first step to its being spoken of as a thing not to be tolerated. . . . He was from the opening of this battle under very little doubt concerning its end. Wealth and the spirit of the age, going, as they usually do go, hand in hand, may be despised but they cannot be resisted. Yet he saw that slavery would stand no chance if the moral case against it was allowed to go by default and the South to appear as a land of heartless ogres, taking advantage of legal quibbles in order to stand upon intolerable rights. The constitutional guarantees of slavery could only be maintained if a case for it was shown to exist apart from constitutional guarantees.

* * *

The laws, if they must cater for the negro as a free man, must be choked up with a catalogue of interferences, which would be quite unnecessary if they had only to deal with white men and the white men in their turn had personal responsibility for the black. The question was not whether one race should be free or two, but whether one race should be free or neither. . . .

Calhoun, it must be remembered, defended not the slave trade but slavery. . . . In general he held no brief for the slave trade, for which the first responsibility lay not with the South but with England and the North. His concern was with the problem of the mixed populations which, from whatever cause, were found living side by side—a problem for which a solution had to be found. One is apt perhaps to sympathize too much with him because of the cowardly futility of the answers that were given to his arguments in his day by such men as Lowell and are still given by many of those who write about him. He was told that he was opposing Progress—by which was meant industrial development. . . . As if he did not know that he was running "a tilt at the Spirit of the Age!" As if he was an opportunist party politician, anxious only to find a cry which would bring him back to office. . . . Not until Lincoln was there to be found one who would answer from first principles an argument from first principles. It was the only answer to which Calhoun would have listened.

Yet, at the end of all, one cannot but feel that Calhoun's arguments prove everything but what they profess to prove. They show admirably that Southern civilization would be ruined if abolition were forced on the South at Northern bidding; that, therefore, if Southern civilization were to be preserved, it was essential that for the moment negro slavery be preserved; that Southern civilization must be preserved in order that America should be saved from the industrial slavery which Northern capitalism would in time impose upon it; that, whenever it came to be abolished, slavery, that ancient institution, would have to be abolished slowly and without panic; but they do not show that slavery is good "in the abstract." That cannot be. It was right to tolerate slavery then as it is right to tolerate capitalism today, but it was not right to praise it. No institution can "in the abstract" be good which is contrary to reality. Slavery is contrary to reality, because it sets up a social relationship of inequality contrary to the religious relationship of equality and because, denying to the slave class the possibility of property, it bars it from the full responsibility of marriage. It was an unnatural relationship, depriving the slave of his natural right to property and the master of his natural obligation to work.

Calhoun said—and, if one reflects on the condition of industrial England at that date, one must admit that it may well be true—that no manual laborer in the world received as large a return for his work as did the American slave in food and clothing. But, when the Great Nullifier thought that that was a justification of slavery, he showed himself no more intelligent than . . . the Labor Party concerning the benefits of slavery to the working man. Of both the fallacy is the same—that of putting all their eggs into one basket. The Socialist would trust everything to the benevolence of the State—that is, of the politician. Calhoun trusted everything to the benevolence of the slave-owner.

*   *   *

The Early Victorian world was more and more coming to the conclusion that in that sense slavery was not in accordance with the law of nations. On the one hand the only hope of saving slavery lay in a rigid adherence to the letter of the law. For to the unwritten law, the appeal in such a cause would in the nineteenth century be necessarily in vain. Yet, on the other hand, Calhoun was wise enough to see that a scrap of paper, unbacked by moral sentiment, could not avert a revolution. It was the dilemma from which he well knew there was no escape. He is called doctrinaire. If he had been merely doctrinaire he would never have seen the dilemma.

* * *

To most Southerners his fears still seemed exaggerated. He failed to win that unanimous support which might just possibly have caused the North to hesitate and thus have prevented war. . . . In sixteen years' time those who laughed at his fears were to see the negroes parading the streets of Charleston and singing:

> De bottom rail's on top now,
> And we're going to keep it dar.

* * *

His two great rivals, Webster and Clay, survived him by some two years, till they, too, died, leaving to smaller men their ghastly heritage. To Clay, the agile discoverer of the happy, compromising formula, to Webster, the Imperialist, intoxicated by his own rhetoric, their country owes much. But a just posterity would not, I fancy, have given them a place in the company of Calhoun.

Many find it difficult to judge Calhoun fairly because of their prejudice against slavery. It is true that he did think slavery "a positive good" when the best that can be said of it in true morals is that under certain circumstances it is the least harmful of possible arrangements. For that he is to be blamed. Yet his political conduct was based, not on his opinion of slavery, but on the one clear premise that the North, incapable of understanding her traditions, would break the Southern life if she got the chance. The premise granted, all logically follows. His love was for liberty. He had no half-wit's ambition to extend slavery to distant lands for its own sake. He wished New Mexico to be slave only in order that South Carolina might remain independent.

Whatever to be our judgment upon his wisdom, the fair historian will say that Calhoun—the later and purer Calhoun, at any rate—was not a man to "turn a coat to decorate a coat," that he never stooped either to flattery or to abuse, to deceive others or to deceive himself, and that these gifts are rare among politicians. Yet, if the premise of his life was false and ridiculous, we must add that here was a verbose alarmist for whose rhetoric the world has had to pay dearly. If, on the other hand, that premise was true, his place, though he was neither impeccable nor infallible, is yet in the first rank of American statesmen. And true it surely was. The new spirit of the age was against him. That spirit he saw as a whole and challenged as a whole. A people, he thought, must live upon its traditions or perish, and industrial capitilism, whose very advertisement was that it was daily changing man's material condition of life, was the enemy.

The old Southern slavery had been, at least, one of the institutions of a stable society. The new industrial slavery was to be mere brute force acting upon chaos. It had been a dogma of the Jeffersonian political philosophy to be intensely suspicious of an industrialism which replaced thought by superficial culture, democracy by hypnosis, and did violence to reason in holding up wealth rather than happiness as the end of man. For the first seventy years of independent America the normal American thought of his country as erected in protest against this disorder of the will which made men in Europe clamor always for a higher material standard of living, and which must of its nature—since matter is limited and appetite unlimited— lead finally to disaster. Since the Civil War it has been thought normal in America, as in England, that man should desire and should be invited to desire as much material wealth as he can get. Calhoun, in his time, saw growing up that new spirit of the age which thought of appetite as a thing merely to be indulged, not merely as a thing to be feared, watched, and controlled. He saw disaster in the growth of that spirit. Was he not enormously right in his foresight? How much understanding of that old Southern life would he have found in the new generations of Henry Fords and Carnegies and Rockefellers? And is the day so very far distant when the new slaves of the North, doomed to slavery, because a man, though he be called a voter and a citizen, who thinks material things more important than freedom, lacks a philosophy which will prevent him from selling his freedom for material things—when these new slaves will read again, perhaps with despair yet nevertheless with understanding, the works and speeches of a great gentleman who never feared to call a spade a spade and a slave a slave?

Webster said of him in a funeral epigram, more exactly true perhaps than its author guessed, that he was "a Senator of Rome, when Rome survived." The phrase is perfect. Jefferson fought against the Christian revelation. To Calhoun, the confident Unitarian, it never occurred to accept it. He, in this no more typical of the South than Jefferson, was a pre-Christian. His was the spirit of those great men, lords, who knew neither anger nor laughter nor injustice, who gave to the world all that mere man can give and who fell in the hour when the world came dimly to guess that what mere man could give was not enough; who, themselves possessing a passion for the Public Thing, were willing to confer on the Empire which they ruled, order, prosperity, administration, roads, everything which the subject could ask—save only the citizenship of Rome. Calhoun held these truths to be self-evident—that all men were born equal and that negroes were not men.

14

Charles M. Wiltse: What Manner of Man?[1]

"Mr. Calhoun's death has deified his opinions," wrote a Northern jurist in June of 1850, "and he is therefore more dangerous dead than living." The choice of adjective is significant. For the last twenty years or more of his life Calhoun's views as to the nature and limits of the government of the United States were regarded by a growing body of his countrymen as "dangerous." Dangerous to the Union, they would have explained, but that was not really what they meant. Calhoun's ideas were dangerous because they threatened the growth and prosperity of the Northern states, the spread of industrialism with its quickly mounting profits, the rapid conquest and exploitation of the continent. They were dangerous not because they challenged the existing order of things but because they would tend to make that order permanent and inhibit change.

Calhoun was as sincerely anxious to preserve the Union as any of his critics, but he wanted to preserve it as he had known it in the days of the Virginia Dynasty. His model was Jefferson, but he built on only one facet of the Jeffersonian tradition, enlarging the doctrine of the Kentucky Resolutions of 1798 into a complete philosophy of government. Intelligent, sincere, incorruptible, in many ways a man of prophetic vision, Calhoun was both a magnificent and a tragic figure, battling to maintain the economic prosperity of an agrarian world in the face of the industrial revolution.

It was inevitable that men who held his ideas to be dangerous would come in time to question his motives. The single-minded zeal and ingenuity with which he fought could not fail to make enemies; and his defense of slavery, by-product though it was, lent a moral stigma to his cause that made hostile evaluation certain. His influence, both as statesman and as thinker, was deep and lasting, and was freely acknowledged in his own time, but his contemporaries disagreed almost violently as to whether its tendency was good or evil. He sym-

[1] From Charles M. Wiltse, *John Calhoun: Sectionalist* (New York, 1968), pp. 479–84. Reprinted by permission of the author.

bolized a basic conflict between two widely different forms of society, and so he was and still remains a controversial figure.

Immediately following Calhoun's death and throughout the next decade interpretations of his career and influence, both publicly and privately expressed, were as far apart as the poles. There were Northern intellectuals who lamented his passing but thought the course of his later years disastrous to the country, while leaders of thought in the South regarded his death as breaking the last link with the political ideals of the Revolution. It was possible for Southerners like Henry S. Foote to charge him with a conscious wish to disrupt the Union, and for Northerners like William Plumer to bracket him with Adams, Webster, and Clay as one of the great men of his time. Reactions to him were emotional, conditioned by personal relationships, by place of residence and economic ties, by ambitions thwarted or advanced through his intervention or the impact of his thought.

As the South rushed headlong toward the ultimate test of Calhoun's logic, opinions as to his motives and the direction of his influence became still more sharply divided. The South, as plans for a Confederacy of her own took firmer shape, came to look on the great Nullifier not as the unwilling prophet but as the active partisan of secession, while the North, with the twisted history of Blair and Benton for confirmation, laid at his door all the evils of the rising sectional conflict. Jefferson Davis, when he took leave of the Senate in January 1861, was at pains to clarify the distinction between Calhoun's position and his own, but it was far too late to convince men inflamed by decades of sectional hostility that the South Carolina Senator had sought only to preserve the Union. Though ten years dead he still personified the slave states, and the slave states were in rebellion. The Northern press, with the license of war, built up the case for his long-standing treason, and survivors of the Jacksonian days like Blair and Kendall and James A. Hamilton, reinterpreted the partisan struggles of the past in the light of the ultimate result.

When hostile armies faced each other in the field at last Calhoun's doctrines, consciously distorted on the one side and imperfectly understood on the other, were accepted by North and South alike as the intellectual genesis of the Confederacy, and they did not survive the final test of battle. The sovereignty passed once and for all from the states to the national government, and Calhoun became to an embittered people the symbol of defeat and destruction. The war had been fought in defense of his ideas, and in the eyes of those who had lost their homes and their loved ones, the responsibility was his.

The ground was thus prepared for the publication of Adams' diary in the 1870's, and for the bitter condemnation of Von Holst in the next decade. It was not until 1900, when the first volume of Calhoun's correspondence was issued under the aegis of the American Historical Association, that it became possible to penetrate the emotionalism of fratricidal war and consider what manner of man this was who aroused such abiding passions in so many breasts.

The years of Calhoun's active political life—roughly from 1810 to 1850—were years of expansion and change more rapid and more sweeping than any the world had previously known. It was during this period that the shift from an agrarian to an industrial economy was assured, with all that shift implied in the evolution of social and political institutions. It was a period of intellectual ferment in which the old mercantilist and planter world was cracking beneath the mighty blows of industrial capitalism and technological change. The Constitution of the United States represented the best in seventeenth and eighteenth-century political thought, but without reinterpretation it could never have survived the first half century of its existence. The strong national government against which Calhoun fought so long and so ingeniously was the only kind of government that could exercise jurisdiction over an economy wealthy and powerful beyond the wildest imaginings of the founding fathers, but it was nothing inherent in the American idea, or in the Anglo-Saxon race, or in the continental sweep of the environment that brought about the ultimate centralization of power. It was not the decisions of John Marshall nor the arguments of Webster, but the industrial revolution itself that won the day. The enduring bonds of union were not a common heritage nor even a common speech, but the steamboat, the railroad, the telegraph, and all the scientific progeny that followed.

The economic and cultural differences between North and South, had it not been for the development of rapid communication, would undoubtedly have become greater rather than less. The period between the American Revolution and the Civil War was one of sociological differentiation, such as had come about in Europe following the breakup of the Roman Empire. But for the technological advances of the early nineteenth century the process would probably have run its course and the continent would have seen not two or three but a dozen nations, each with its own national characteristics and economy.

It was a process familiar enough to Calhoun's generation. The American Revolution, the French Revolution, the Napoleonic wars, the revolt of the Spanish colonies in the Western Hemisphere, the Texan revolution, and the European uprisings of 1848 all occurred within the span of a long lifetime. To those who lived through any substantial portion of this period, governments must certainly have appeared to be unstable things and regional self-determination the natural order of events. The *Declaration of Independence* had stated the case as clearly as it would ever be stated, and it was inevitable that Southerners who felt themselves oppressed should compare their grievances with those against which their fathers had rebelled. They were undoubtedly correct in their contention that the economic impact of the tariffs of 1828 and 1842 was more damaging to the cotton states than ever the taxes of George III had been to the colonies, and the antislavery agitation, in economic terms, was more disastrous still.

Calhoun was the most articulate and clearest-headed of Southern spokesmen but his influence was consistently thrown to the side of union. He used the real grievances of the planters not to inspire a separatist revolt but to consolidate a pressure bloc whose aim was to secure concessions from the stronger interest. In 1833 and again in 1846 he did secure modification of the tariff, but the antislavery agitation, because of the moral base on which it rested, was not to be stopped that way. It is true that Calhoun's logic justified the ultimate secession of the South; true also that the very stubbornness of his defense of slavery intensified the zeal of the abolitionists and increased their political power. It is not likely, however, that the result would have been materially changed had he never lived. He did not create but only formulated and expressed the attitude of the planter class to which he belonged, seeking always to direct Southern discontent into nonviolent channels.

In the process he developed and refined a constitutional doctrine that would in itself be an adequate defense of the old agrarian order, but it was a doctrine incompatible with the powerful national state required by the industrial economy of the North. This is not to say that Calhoun's reasoning was in any way responsible for the Civil War, even though the end product was the supremacy of the Federal Government. The basic cause of the sectional conflict was a fundamental antagonism between two divergent economies, and as long as the cause remained the conflict was bound to come, sooner or later, no matter how the two contestants rationalized their positions.

Calhoun's genius lay in his awareness of the problem his country faced, and his greatest contribution was his long and patient effort to explain it in terms that would make a peaceable solution possible.

The United States was the first great modern nation in which agriculture and industry were both major interests. Calhoun more than any other man drove home the point that policies designed to foster and encourage the one would be ruinous to the other, and we have come at last, though by a different route, to his position. We have recognized the necessity, in a nation embracing many economic interests, for equalizing what he called the burdens and bounties of government. We have done it by direct action through taxation and subsidies, and in the process we have made the central government powerful beyond Calhoun's most gloomy fears; but we have at least recognized the problem with which he struggled, and we have arrived at a solution, however tentative, within the framework of the Constitution—not the Constitution he so painstakingly limited lest the society he cherished be destroyed, but one better suited to the needs of a more complex age and perhaps not less responsive to the welfare of those who are governed by it.

The federation of sovereign states that seemed to Calhoun the only practical way to reconcile the conflicting demands of agriculture and industry was essentially static, without adequate room for the development of a dynamic society. The concurrent veto was negative, defensive, designed to preserve the order of things as they were. In action it could only obstruct, until obstruction became intolerable and had to be swept aside. Thoroughgoing conservative that he was, Calhoun came at last to place security for his class above all other considerations, and when security becomes an end in itself the society is doomed.

In his rejection of the democratic dogma, and in his failure to appreciate the moral values in the antislavery crusade, Calhoun was following out the premises of his own mechanistic theory of society. His estimate of human nature was low, but his analysis of the political process is still largely valid, and is nowhere better illustrated than in his own career. His defense of the minority against the weight of numbers is timeless in its application, and his insistence that the power of government must somehow be controlled is a universal condition of human freedom.

For himself and in his own time his path was marked by repeated failures, but his place in history cannot be determined in terms of his own political fortunes. As statesman he came to grips with the basic problems of government, and clarified the issues for a half century of partisan conflict. As political theorist he showed more clearly than any other American has ever done how the political process works.

15

Richard Hofstadter: The Marx of the Master Class[1]

The idea that Calhoun was a pre-Marxist originated in a brilliant essay by Richard B. Current, "John C. Calhoun, Philosopher of Reaction," Antioch Review, III (Summer, 1943), 223–24. Wherever Southern Bourbons gather, Current contended, Calhoun's ghost lingers, and the key to his career was his concept of the class struggle. Hofstadter builds on Current's foundation.

Jackson led through force of personality, not intellect; his successors in the White House were remarkable for neither, and yielded preeminence to Congressional politicians. Of the three greatest, Clay, Webster, and Calhoun, the last showed the most striking mind. His problem, that of defending a minority interest in a democracy, offered the toughest challenge to fresh thinking.

*　　*　　*

Calhoun, representing a conscious minority with special problems, brought new variations into American political thinking. Although his concepts of nullification and the concurrent voice have little more than antiquarian interest for the twentieth-century mind, he also set forth a system of social analysis that is worthy of considerable respect. Calhoun was one of a few Americans of his age—Richard Hildreth and Orestes Brownson were others—who had a keen sense for social structure and class forces. Before Karl Marx published the *Communist Manifesto,* Calhoun laid down an analysis of American politics and the sectional struggle which foreshadowed some of the seminal ideas of Marx's system. A brilliant if narrow dialectician, probably the last American statesman to do any primary political thinking, he

[1] From Richard Hofstadter, "John C. Calhoun: The Marx of the Master Class," in *The American Political Tradition* (New York, 1948), pp. 68–69, 82–83, 88–91.

placed the central ideas of "scientific" socialism in an inverted framework of moral values and produced an arresting defense of reaction, a
sort of intellectual Black Mass.

*   *   *

In 1837 he wrote to Hammond that he had had "no conception
that the lower class had made such great progress to equality and
independence" as Hammond had reported. "Modern society seems
to me to be rushing to some new and untried condition." "What I
dread," he confessed to his daughter Anna in 1846, "is that progress
in political science falls far short of progress in that which relates to
matter, and which may lead to convulsions and revolutions, that may
retard, or even arrest the former." During the peak of the Jacksonian
bank war he wrote to his son James that the views of many people
in the North were inclining toward Southern conceptions. They
feared not only Jackson's power, but "the needy and corrupt in their
own section. They begin to feel what I have long foreseen, that they
have more to fear from their own people than we from our slaves."

In such characteristic utterances there is discernible a rough parallel
to several ideas that were later elaborated and refined by Marx: the
idea of pervasive exploitation and class struggle in history; a labor
theory of value and of a surplus appropriated by the capitalists; the
concentration of capital under capitalistic production; the fall of
working class conditions to the level of subsistence; the growing revolt of the laboring class against the capitalists; the prediction of
social revolution. The difference was that Calhoun proposed that no
revolution should be allowed to take place. To forestall it he suggested consistently—over a period of years—what Richard Current
has called "planter-capitalist collaboration against the class enemy."
In such a collaboration the South, with its superior social stability,
had much to offer as a conservative force. In return, the conservative
elements in the North should be willing to hold down abolitionist
agitation; and they would do well to realize that an overthrow of
slavery in the South would prepare the ground for social revolution
in the North.

> There is and always has been [he said in the Senate] in an advanced
> stage of wealth and civilization, a conflict between labor and capital.
> The condition of society in the South exempts us from the disorders
> and dangers resulting from this conflict; and which explains why it is
> that the political conditions of the slave-holding states has been so
> much more stable and quiet than that of the North. . . . The expe-

rience of the next generation will fully test how vastly more favorable
our condition of society is to that of other sections for free and stable
institutions, provided we are not disturbed by the interference of
others, or shall . . . resist promptly and successfully such interference.

. . . In 1836 Calhoun had pointed out to "the sober and con-
siderate" Northerners

> who have a deep stake in the existing institutions of the country that
> the assaults which are now directed against the institutions of the
> Southern States may be very easily directed against those which uphold
> their own property and security. A very slight modification of the
> arguments used against the institutions [of the South] would make
> them equally effectual against the institutions of the North, including
> banking, in which so vast an amount of its property and capital is
> invested.

In 1847 he again reminded Northern conservatives how much interest they had "in upholding and preserving the equilibrium of the
slaveholding states." "Let gentlemen then be warned that while
warring on us, they are warring on themselves."

*   *   *

Far in advance of the event, he forecast an alliance between Northern conservatives and Southern reactionaries, which has become one
of the most formidable aspects of American politics. The South, its
caste system essentially intact, has proved to be for an entire century
more resistant to change than the North, its influence steadily exerted
to retard serious reform and to curb the power of Northern labor.
Caste prejudice and political conservatism had made the South a
major stronghold of American capitalism.

But prescient and ingenious as Calhoun was, he made critical mis-
calculations for the sectional struggle of his own time. He had a
remarkable sense for the direction of social evolution, but failed to
measure its velocity. His fatal mistake was to conclude that the conflict between labor and capital would come to a head before the
conflict between capital and the Southern planter. Marx out of opti-
mism and Calhoun out of pessimism both overestimated the revolutionary capacities of the working class. It was far easier to reconcile
the Northern masses to the profit system than Calhoun would ever
admit. He failed to see that the expanding Northern free society, by
offering broad opportunities to the lower and middle classes, provided
itself with a precious safety valve for popular discontents. He also

failed to see that the very restlessness which he considered the North's weakness was also a secret of its strength. "The mainspring to progress," he realized, "is the desire of individuals to better their condition," but he could not admit how much more intensely free society stimulated that essential desire in its working population than his cherished slave system with its "thirty lashes well laid on."

Calhoun, in brief, failed to appreciate the staying power of capitalism. At the very time when it was swinging into its period of most hectic growth he spoke as though it had already gone into decline. The stirrings of the Jackson era particularly misled him; mass discontent, which gained further opportunities for the common man in business and politics, and thus did so much in the long run to strengthen capitalism, he misread as the beginning of a revolutionary upsurge. Calhoun was, after all, an intense reactionary, and to the reactionary ear every whispered criticism of the elite classes has always sounded like the opening shot of an uprising.

*   *   *

Ironically, for a long time Northern labor was ideologically closer than Northern capital to the planters. The workers had little sympathy for abolitionism, but responded with interest when Southern politicians unleashed periodic assaults on Northern wage slavery. When Francis W. Pickens, one of Calhoun's own lieutenants, rose in the House in the fall of 1837 to point out that the planters stood in relation to Northern capital "precisely in the same situation as the laborer of the North" and that they were "the only class of capitalists . . . which, as a class, are identified with the laborers of the country." Ely Moore, a labor spokesman, endorsed his position. And eight years after Calhoun's death, when James H. Hammond lashed out in a famous speech against "wage slavery," he received many letters of thanks from Northern workers for exposing their condition. Calhoun himself, organizing his presidential drive between 1842 and 1844, found strong support among many members of the former left wing of Northern democracy. Fitzwilliam Byrdsall, ardent democrat and historian of the Locofocos, wrote to him from New York City that "the radical portion of the Democratic party here, to whom free suffrage is dear and sacred, is the very portion most favorable to you." Calhoun had not long before expected this sort of man to frighten the capitalists into the arms of the planters!

The essence of Calhoun's mistake as a practical statesman is that he tried to achieve a static solution for a dynamic situation. The North, stimulated by invention and industry and strengthened by a tide of immigration, was growing in population and wealth, filling the West, and building railroads that bound East and West together. No concurrent majority, nor any other principle embodied in a parchment, could stem the tide that was measured every ten years in the census returns. William H. Seward touched upon the South's central weakness in his speech of March 11, 1850, when he observed that what the Southerners wanted was "a *political* equilibrium. Every political equilibrium requires a physical equilibrium to rest upon, and is valueless without it." In the face of all realities, the Southerners kept demanding that equality of territory and approximate equality of populations be maintained. "And this," taunted Seward, "must be perpetual!"

Moreover, the Calhoun dialectic was so starkly reactionary in its implications that it became self-defeating. There was disaster even for the South in the premise that every civilized society must be built upon a submerged and exploited labor force—what Hammond called a "mud-sill" class. *If* there must always be a submerged and exploited class at the base of society, and *if* the Southern slaves, as such a class, were better off than Northern free workers, and *if* slavery was the safest and most durable base on which to found political institutions, then there seemed to be no reason why *all* workers, white or black, industrial or agrarian, should not be slave rather than free. Calhoun shrank from this conclusion, but some Southerners did not. . . .

Calhoun could see and expound very plausibly every weakness of Northern society, but his position forced him to close his eyes to the vulnerability of the South. Strong as he was on logical coherence, he had not the most elementary moral consistency. Here it is hard to follow those who, like Professor Wiltse, find in him "the supreme champion of minority rights and interests everywhere." It is true that Calhoun superbly formulated the problem of the relation between majorities and minorities, and his work at this point may have the permanent significance for political theory that is often ascribed to it. But how can the same value be assigned to his practical solutions? Not in the slightest was he concerned with minority rights as they are chiefly of interest to the modern liberal mind—the rights of dissenters to express unorthodox opinions, of the individual conscience against the State, least of all of ethnic minorities. At bottom he was not interested in any minority that was not a propertied minority. The concurrent majority itself was a device without relevance to the protection of dissent, but designed specifically to protect a vested interest of considerable power. Even within the South, Calhoun had not the slightest desire to protect intellectual minorities, critics, and dissenters. Professor Clement Eaton, in his *Freedom of Thought in the Old South,* places him first among those politicians who "created stereotypes in the minds of the Southern people that produced intolerance." Finally, it was minority privileges rather than rights that he really proposed to protect. He wanted to give to the minority not merely a proportionate but an *equal* voice with the majority in determining public policy. He would have found incomprehensible the statement of William H. Roane, of Virginia, that he had "never thought that [minorities] had any other *Right* than that of freely, peaceably, & *legally* converting themselves into a *majority* whenever they can." This elementary right Calhoun was prompt to deny to any minority, North or South, that disagreed with him on any vital question. In fact, his first great speeches on the slavery question were prompted by his attempt to deny the right of petition to a minority.

Calhoun was a minority spokesman in a democracy, a particularist in an age of nationalism, a slaveholder in an age of advancing liberties, and an agrarian in a furiously capitalistic country. Quite understandably he developed a certain perversity of mind. It became his peculiar faculty, the faculty of a brilliant but highly abstract and isolated intellect, to see things that other men never dreamt of and to deny what was under his nose, to forecast with uncanny insight several major trends of the future and remain all but oblivious of the actualities of the present.

16

Peter Drucker: Calhoun's Pluralism[1]

To find an adequate analysis of the principle of government by sectional and interest compromise we have to go back almost a hundred years to John C. Calhoun and to his two political treatises published after his death in 1852. Absurd, you will say, for it is practically an axiom of American history that Calhoun's political theories, subtle, even profound though they may have been, were reduced to absurdity and irrelevance by the Civil War. Yet, this "axiom" is nothing but a partisan vote of the Reconstruction Period. Of course, the specific occasion for which Calhoun formulated his theories, the Slavery issue, has been decided; and for the constitutional veto power of the states over national legislation, by means of which Calhoun proposed to formalize the principle of sectional and interest compromise, was substituted in actual practice the much more powerful and much more elastic but extra-constitutional and extra-legal veto power of sections, interests and pressure groups in Congress and within the parties. But *his basic principle itself: that every major interest in the country, whether regional, economic, or religious, is to possess a veto power on political decisions directly affecting it,* the principle which Calhoun called—rather obscurely—*"the rule of concurrent majority,"* has become the organizing principle of American politics. And it is precisely this principle that is under fire today.

What makes Calhoun so important as the major key to the understanding of American politics, is not just that he saw the importance in American political life of sectional and interest pluralism; other major analysts of our government, Tocqueville, for instance, or Bryce or Wilson, saw that too. But Calhoun, perhaps alone, saw in it more than a rule of expediency, imposed by the country's size and justifiable by results, if at all. He saw in it a basic principle of free government.

*　　*　　*

[1] From Peter F. Drucker, "A Key to American Politics: Calhoun's Pluralism," *The Review of Politics* (October, 1948), 412–26.

Sectional and interest pluralism has molded all American political institutions. It is the method—entirely unofficial and extra-constitutional—through which the organs of government are made to function, through which leaders are selected, policies developed, men and groups organized for the conquest and management of political power. In particular it is the explanation for the most distinctive features of the American political system: the way in which the Congress operates, the way in which major government departments are set up and run, the qualifications for "eligibility" as a candidate for elective office, and the American party structure.

To all foreign observers of Congress two things have always remained mysterious: the distinction between the official party label and the "blocs" which cut across party lines; and the power and function of the Congressional Committees. And most Americans though less amazed by the phenomena are equally baffled.

The "blocs"—the "Farm Bloc," the "Friends of Labor in the Senate," the "Business Groups," etc.—are simply the expression of the basic tenet of sectional and interest pluralism that major interests have a veto power on legislation directly affecting them. For this reason they must cut across party lines—that is, lines expressing the numerical rather than the "concurrent" majority. And because these blocs have (a) only a negative veto, and (b) only on measures directly affecting them, they cannot in themselves be permanent groupings replacing the parties. They must be loosely organized; and one and the same member of Congress must at different times vote with different blocs. The strength of the "blocs" does not rest on their numbers but on the basic mores of American politics which grant every major interest group a limited self-determination—as expressed graphically in the near-sanctity of a senatorial "filibuster." The power of the "Farm Bloc" for instance, does not rest on the numerical strength of the rural vote—a minority vote even in the Senate with its disproportionate representation of the thinly populated agricultural states—but on its "strategic" strength, that is on its being the spokesman for a recognized major interest.

* * *

It is not only Congress but every individual member of Congress himself who is expected to operate according to the "rule of concurrent majority." He is considered both a representative of the American people and responsible to the national interest and a delegate of his constituents and responsible to their particular interests. Wherever the immediate interests of his constituents are not in question, he is to be a statesman; wherever their conscience or their pocketbooks are affected, he is to be a business agent. . . .

The mystery of "eligibility"—the criteria which decides who will make a promising candidate for public office—which has baffled so many foreign and American observers, Bryce for instance—also traces back to the "rule of the concurrent majority." Eligibility simply means that a candidate must not be unacceptable to any major interest, religious or regional group within the electorate; it is primarily a negative qualification. Eligibility operates on all levels and applies to all elective offices. It has been brilliantly analyzed in "Boss" Flynn's *You're the Boss.* His classical example is the selection of Harry Truman as Democratic vice-presidential candidate in 1944. Truman was "eligible" rather than Wallace, Byrnes or Douglas precisely because he was unknown; because he was neither Easterner nor Westerner nor Southerner, because he was neither New Deal nor Conservative, etc., in short because he had no one trait strong enough to offend anybody anywhere.

But the central institution based on sectional pluralism is the American party. Completely extra-constitutional, the wonder and the despair of every foreign observer who cannot fit into any of his concepts of political life, the American party (rather than the states) has become the instrument to realize Calhoun's "rule of the concurrent majority."

In stark contrast to the parties of Europe, the American party has no program and no purpose except to organize divergent groups for the common pursuit and conquest of power. Its unity is one of action, not of beliefs. Its only rule is to attract—or at least not to repel—the largest possible number of groups. It must, by definition, be acceptable equally to the right and the left, the rich and the poor, the farmer and the worker, the Protestant and the Catholic, the native and the foreign-born. It must be able to rally Mr. Rankin of Mississippi and Mr. Marcantonio of New York—or Senator Flanders and Colonel McCormick—behind the same presidential candidate and the same "platform."

As soon as it cannot appeal at least to a minority in every major group (as soon, in other words, as it provokes the veto of one section, interest or class) a party is in danger of disintegration. Whenever a party loses its ability to fuse sectional pressures and class interests into one national policy—both parties just before the Civil War, the Republican Party before its reorganization by Mark Hanna, both parties again today—the party system (and with it the American political system altogether) is in crisis. It is, consequently, not that Cal-

houn was repudiated by the Civil War which is the key to the understanding of American politics but that he has become triumphant
since.

The apparent victors, the "Radical Republicans," Thaddeus Stevens,
Seward, Chief Justice Chase, were out to destroy not only slavery and
states rights but the "rule of the concurrent majority" itself. And the
early Republican Party—before the Civil War and in the Reconstruction period—was indeed determined to substitute principle for interest
as the lodestar of American political life. But in the end it was the
political thought of convinced pluralists such as Abraham Lincoln
and Andrew Johnson rather than the ideologies of the Free Soilers
and Abolitionists which molded the Republican Party. And ever since,
the major developments of American politics have been based on
Calhoun's principle. To this the United States owes the strength as
well as the weaknesses of its political system.

17
Margaret L. Coit: Calhoun as an Agrarian Nationalist[1]

To him, the Union seemed a fragile thing, too deli
cately wrought to stand "on the cold calculation of interest, alone
. . . too weak to stand political convulsions. . . . I feel no dispo
sition to deny," he had said, as early as 1814, that if the majority
ceased "to consult the general interest . . . it would be more danger
ous than a factious minority." Party "rage," he saw as the great "weak
ness of all free governments," and precedent as scarcely less dangerous
"It is not unusual," he had said two years earlier, "for executive
power, unknown to those who exercise it, to make encroachments
. . . What has been the end of all free governments, but open force
or the gradual undermining of the legislative by the executive power.
The peculiar construction of ours by no means exempts us from this
evil. . . . Were it not for the habits of the people we would naturally
tend that way." What he desired was "the whole" of the govern
ment in "full possession of its primitive powers, but all of the parts
confined to their respective spheres." So he spoke in 1812; and again
in 1833 and 1848.

Fragmentary as these observations are, their remarkable prophecies
alone make them worthy of serious study. More important, they offer
conclusive proof of an assertion that "if the young Calhoun had been
asked to define the relations of the State to the General Government
he would have used language not very different from that with which
he was afterwards to defy Webster or Jackson." Clearly, what he was
already defining as "the conflict between the States and General
Government" was not yet uppermost in his mind. Nevertheless, he
had said enough to show that basically the Calhoun of 1815 and the
Calhoun of 1833 were one man.

For eighty years historians have divided Calhoun's public career
into two sharply defined sections: one, nationalist, the other, sec
tionalist. This is an oversimplification. Basically Calhoun was a

[1] From Margaret L. Coit, *John C. Calhoun: American Portrait* (Boston: Hough
ton Mifflin Company, 1950), pp. 104–105, 114–15, 227, 518–21, 524–28.

nce a nationalist and a sectionalist from the beginning to the end f his career. In 1815 he represented a majority; by 1833 those who hought as he did were in the minority, which explains where the lifference lay. In 1815 he was as representative of the frontier farmers s he later became of the planting South; but in 1815 the frontier tretched all the way from rock-tipped Maine to the Alabama border. .ike other nationalists, Daniel Webster included, Calhoun was al-/ays to demand first protection for his immediate constituency.

Now, despite John Taylor's warnings, Calhoun saw no interest nimical to that Southern life he loved. The difference between the :alhoun of 1815 and the Calhoun of 1833 is a matter of knowledge, ot of philosophy. Bitter experience divides the confident young •atriot who had yet to learn the dangers of nationalism and the worn-•ut statesman in whom hope was almost dead. For it is "not incon-istent that a man should allow much freedom to a partner whom he till trusts, which he would be reluctant to allow to one of whom he ias come to be suspicious."

To Calhoun, the future was a "could be," not a "would be." He ailed to heed his own warnings. He trusted his heart, not his head. Ie had faith and hope; he had confidence in the "virtue and intel-igence of the American people." Later, he would change his mind. ▲ nationalistic America, which practiced as well as preached "the eneral welfare" could conceivably have endured on the principle f majority rule; but a nation which had divided into states, regions, nd groups must find other means for that "justice" which Calhoun n 1813 defined as the "prime objective of government" to survive. t would be Calhoun's task to seek ways of both restraining and atisfying the "cold" calculations which he had predicted might de-troy the Union, so that, in disproof of his own predictions, the Union /ould endure.

*　　*　　*

Despite the routine that absorbed Calhoun in those post-war years, •e never lost sight of his goal. The "broadening Union" was always oremost in his thoughts. He gave expression to his views in an ad-lress remarkable for its link between the "national" and the "sec-ional" Calhoun of the historian's creation.

Here are the phrases so often on his lips in the future: "the selfish nstincts of our nature . . . the rival jealousies of the States." These re the forces which he increasingly saw as threatening the Union— he forces of diversity, the clashing interest of the sections. Now, as lways, liberty was foremost with him—in fact, he saw the Union as

founded to preserve liberty. When sectional interests should become
so diverse as to threaten the liberty of a group of states to follow
their own pattern of life, then, the Carolinian foresaw, the Union
would fall. In 1816, as in his last years of life, every energy was
dedicated to preventing this catastrophe—to seeking methods by which
diverse interests might be reconciled—forces which would prevent
any states or sections with a numerical majority from thrusting their
will upon a minority section.

Calhoun's objectives and fears in 1816 were the objectives of a
lifetime; he would change only in his methods. His goal was constant
to preserve the Union, and to hold back all forces which might rend
the Union apart. The great size of our country, he told Congress
"exposes us to the greatest of all calamities, *next to the loss of liberty*
—disunion. . . ."

*"What is necessary for the common good may apparently be op
posed to the interest of particular sections. It must be submitted to
as the condition of our greatness."*

Here, indeed, is the crux of the charge that Calhoun was incon
sistent, that the Great Nationalist of 1816 right-about-faced to become
the Great Sectionalist of the eighteen-forties. The man who in youth
voiced these words would thirty years later become the leader of the
minority South's struggle to maintain her own way of life against
the majority of the nation.

But Calhoun did not use words loosely. Young as he was, he was a
realist. Already he had sensed the dangers to political freedom in the
wage-slavery of the workshops. Already he was aware of the danger
when "attachment to party becomes stronger than attachment to
country." His thinking deepened and expanded with the passing
years, but it is hard to believe that the whole basis of his political
thought overturned. The key to the dilemma is in the phrase, "What
is necessary for the common good."

For what Calhoun saw as the common good, he had defined clearly
if negatively, in his speech, pointing out "the greatest of all calamities
next to the loss of liberty—disunion." Already Calhoun saw what
Webster saw, years later, that to the common good liberty *and* union
were the ideal. To Calhoun, liberty meant the right of an individual
a state, a section, or "an interest," to manage its own affairs—to adopt
its own "peculiar institutions," unless these institutions threatened
the common good. In all sincerity, Calhoun never deemed the peculiar
institutions of the South, either slavery or the agrarian way of life
incompatible with the "common good," or endangering either the
liberty or the union of the country as a whole.

* * *

With their roots sunk in the soil, up-countrymen and Charlestonians alike were united in their fear of the Northern factory system which "killed man's inner glow." The North could boast of the kind of freedom that saw the mill-hand rise to the mill presidency in a single generation. But what of the hapless thousands who sweated on the workbenches all their lives long for ninety cents a day? Men should control their own time, contended the Southern leaders, develop their own capabilities, rather than speed their bodies and minds to the tempo of machinery. Hence, they clung to agriculture, basing their society on preference rather than reason. Even the Charlestonians had chosen the agrarian life. It was not the merchants and businessmen, the "year-round" citizenry who gave Charleston its peculiar flavor, but the rice and cotton planters, who lived in the city only three or four months in the year. The representative Charlestonian was an equally representative planter.

In the South the values were set from the top, unlike the North and later the West, where the people made their own way of life, and values were lowered for popular consumption. In the South civilization was a stabilized ideal toward which all white men could aspire, but its ultimate goals they neither could nor wanted to change. For in the South aristocracy was not the possession of the chosen few; it was the ideal of the whole. This was a civilization upon which strong men could make their imprint: aristocratic in its ideal; democratic in the availability of the ideal.

What was America—Northern opportunity or Southern self-realization, Northern democracy or Southern republicanism? Had the South abandoned the American idea, or had the American idea abandoned the South? North and South the gulf was widening. "Washington left a . . . pure republic . . . it has now settled down into a democracy," noted Captain Marryat in 1839. Only in the South did that form of government survive in which men chose from the highest those free to think for the lowest.

* * *

Behind him when he died, unfinished but blocked out, were his two books—*A Disquisition on Government* and *A Discourse on the Constitution of the United States*—to which he had literally given his last days and almost his last hours. Upon them his claim to fame is assured. For here, stripped of the day-to-day issues of his own time, is the essence of his entire political philosophy, the sum of all his living and thinking. Here is what latter-day critics would hail as perhaps the most powerful defense of minority rights in a democracy ever written.

It was a somber prophecy for later times, a haunted warning for his own. Yet in his own day it was neither heeded nor understood. The South Carolina Legislature issued the work, together with his speeches, in a *de luxe* edition which was placed in reverence on Southern shelves, but how wide a reading audience those six abstract, closely written volumes obtained during the years of war and strife, it is not difficult to surmise. As for the victorious North, it had no desire to read or heed the warnings of the vanquished. Yet, as has been observed, when a man like Calhoun puts his last breath into a warning for his people, the people themselves are the losers if they do not hear what he has to say.

The first book is superior to the second, which is diffuse, repetitive, clearly showing the illness of its author. Yet even the second is extraordinary. It is too much to claim, as do the most fervid Southern enthusiasts, that these books rank with Aristotle's, but with the single exception of the *Federalist Papers,* they represent America's most remarkable contribution to political thought.

In the *Disquisition* Calhoun outlined what he conceived to be the principles of government in general, and of democratic government in particular. In the *Discourse* he illustrated these principles by means of the Constitution and the American federal theory—and here is where the difficulties begin. For none knew better than Calhoun how vastly America had outgrown the federal pattern; and that the interests, once represented by states and later by sections, would soon be scattered across the entire country. By 1850, Calhoun had realized that although politically states' rights were a safeguard, economically they were not enough. Von Holst points out how in the end Calhoun repudiated what had been supposed to be his entire political philosophy; fifteen years after his passing, a generation of Southern young men would die in the name of states' rights, mistakenly supposing that they were dying in the name of Calhoun.

For passionate as was Calhoun's love for South Carolina; convinced as he was that the state was the unit upon which America was built, this organization still, to Calhoun, was a means and not an end. He was fighting, not for the original American pattern, but for the general federal theory; but this not even his most devoted admirers could understand. And not the federal theory alone, but the justice which the federal theory was devised to maintain, was to Calhoun the essence of America. America had outgrown states' rights

—the usurpations of majority rule proved this—thus the theory must be reworked upon a new pattern.

This explains the confusion that distorts the second volume of Calhoun's mighty work. How could a country, which had embodied its theory in a pattern, maintain the theory without the pattern? Yet Calhoun's very recognition of this dilemma is the measure of his greatness as a statesman. It was not the Union that mattered so much as the purpose behind it. Calhoun was not doctrinaire; his aim was to make democracy work.

The purpose of his book was threefold: to save the South, to save the Union, to save the federal principles of the Union. All, he knew, were indispensable, one to the other. He knew that 1850 was the last chance for the South and West to rally behind a constitutional amendment which he thought would "protect the South forever against economic exploitation." He knew that ten years later would be too late. Within the Union, unconquered, the South could form a barrier against the final triumph of industrial centralization and unchecked majority rule; without, all would be lost.

Thus, in his last days, with haunted vision and in agony of spirit Calhoun had thrust against the forces which challenged the Union. The right to secede, as a last resort, hopeless as secession might be, he did not deny: "That a State, as a party to the constitutional compact, has the right to secede . . . cannot be denied by anyone who regards the Constitution as a compact—if a power should be inserted by the amending power, which would radically change the character of the system; *or if the former should fail to fulfill the ends for which it was established.*" Yet, practically, he knew that the South's only hope was in the Union.

Calhoun saw the country politically as "a democratic Federal republic, democratic not aristocratic, federal not national . . . of states, not of individuals." He saw it as a government, not of the numerical majority, but of the concurrent majority—with each major group in society having a voice in the legislation affecting it, as in the legislation affecting the whole.

Economically, his ideal was not an agrarian, but a balanced, economy. The numerical supremacy of factory workers over farmers, of industrialists over planters, he considered had nothing to do with the rights and powers belonging to each group. The one was not the slave of the other; all were essential to the maintenance of a sound and healthy economic system.

For Calhoun, America was a protest against the European spirit, against an aristocracy of birth, against the artificial aristocracy of

accumulated wealth "and the decadence of men." The South, although
conservative, static, at odds with the dynamic and expanding North
he saw as the symbol of this protest. Already the South was an
anachronism, a minority voice against the majority will, but still the
last barrier against the rising, middle-class, standardized civilization
which was sweeping the world in the wake of the Industrial Revo
lution.

Future events would prove to many how terribly right he had been.
A century later Harold Laski would find an America committed to
the evaluation of men by what they had rather than what they were—
to the pursuit of wealth rather than of happiness as the chief end of
man.

To Calhoun the American system was an experiment in diversity.
It was based upon the right of peoples to choose their own way of
life, economic and social, and to live it, regardless of the majority
pattern. America's freedom was in her differences. Under the federal
political system, as written, different civilizations, granting that they
could agree on principles involving the common interest and common
safety of all, could live together.

In the South a special civilization had developed. It was a Southern
civilization, common only to that region and representative of it. Yet
it was under the American system that it had grown to fruition; and
it was authentically American.

With the secession of the South, the great American experiment
would be at an end. As a political philosopher and as a patriot
Calhoun could not bear to see it end. Furthermore, in the American
system Calhoun saw principles applicable to the entire world, to all
mankind. One of the earliest advocates of "One World," he was,
however, wise enough to know that there could never be one pattern
of culture for the world. In a world where "progress in matter," as
he had long foreseen, had outstripped moral development, you may
say that you must have one standard of values to exist, but it does
not follow either that you will have the values or continue to exist.
As a practical statesman, Calhoun was not so much interested in
what you have to have, or should have, as in what you could have.

Any government, national or world-wide, that crushes men into a
single pattern, he deemed a despotic government. This was the prin
ciple invoked by every conqueror through time; and for the United
States, for example, to impose on the world one system of industrial
capitalism, whether good or evil, would be adoption of the tyrannical
belief that the world could only exist under one system. Half a
century before Adolf Hitler was born, Calhoun had the wisdom to

know that although men may agree on general principles of safety, a world system based upon one country's concept of freedom, denies others the very right of choice which is essential to freedom.

* * *

Calhoun knew there was no justice without self-determination. It was not democracy when 51% of the people have a moral right to coerce 49%. To put the matter into terms of our day, would there be any moral sanction for the reestablishment of slavery, provided that a majority could be induced to vote for it?

Calhoun, "bolder and more logical than Jefferson," feared centralized government no less than unrestrained industrialism, but he knew it was a *fait accompli* and hence must be recognized and controlled. Again, a realist, he saw that "We must take men as they are, and do the best we can with them. . . . If all were disinterested patriots, there would be no difficulty in running or managing the political machine, and very little credit in doing either."

If a free government could rest only upon the realization of the Christian ideal of brotherhood and unselfishness, then, Calhoun feared, we should never have a free government. Men could be free, however—even with selfish human nature unchanged—if they had but wisdom enough to understand themselves. Self-interest could be the best promoter of compromise. When men realized that their own interests would be lost unless they allowed their fellows to protect themselves, then only would agreements be reached. A democracy based on the principle of the concurrent majority, Calhoun believed, would unite the most conflicting elements "and blend the whole in one common attachment to the country. . . . Each sees and feels that it can best promote its own prosperity by . . . promoting the prosperity of the others." For antipathy and rivalry would be substituted the ideal of "the common good."

* * *

To him the Union had been devised for certain ends, enumerated in the Constitutional Convention. Through the "peculiar Federal structure" of our government, America's freedoms were protected. If ours was a government, not of men, but of law, the Constitution was the ultimate law. If our Union were to endure, then the Constitution could not be used to defeat the ends it had been written to maintain.

So reasoned Calhoun. And so runs the explanation of his lifelong struggle to "restore our government to its original purity and to keep it within the limits of the Constitution." The Constitution, as written, had devised new principles which, evolved, might mean new freedoms for all men. This was the kind of America he fought to preserve. "I don't want to destroy the Union," was his continual cry, "I only wish to make it honest." If he be a disunionist who insists upon constitutional guarantees above the will of the people, upon the ultimate authority of law above men, then Calhoun was a disunionist. Logically, he was right. There is no freedom where a simple majority can dispense with constitutional safeguards. If a popular majority were to become the ultimate law, then, as Jefferson had realized, the Constitution would be so much waste paper. Men could talk of freedom while they violated the constitutional provisions that authorized slavery, but Calhoun knew, only too well, that if constitutional law could be set aside at will to free the blacks, it could as easily be disregarded to enslave the whites.

Despite all the guarantees of its written Constitution, however, none knew better than Calhoun that the United States was far from immune to the dangers that had destroyed all free republics of the past. Totalitarianism was not a word in his vocabulary—oligarchy would have been his nearest approach to it—but he was aware of its meanings nevertheless. In every past age, democracies had drifted steadily toward consolidation, and consolidation meant the destruction of the local rights and freedoms that the republic was created to preserve. Only a federal as opposed to a national system of government could prevent this; and the future colonial subjugation of both the South and West would prove an interesting object lesson to idealists who pinned their faith in mere political democracy without restraints.

*　　*　　*

No justice, Calhoun contended, written constitution or none, could be preserved without restraints. "It is idle, worse than idle, to attempt to distinguish . . . between a government of unlimited powers, and one professedly limited, but with an unlimited right to determine the extent of its powers." Yet such, men were beginning to claim, was the structure of the United States.

He had seen as early as nullification days the error in our Constitution, that the "Federal government contains . . . no provisions by which the powers delegated could be prevented from encroaching on the powers reserved to the several States."

Why has this fundamental omission been made? Calhoun would have said that it was due to a faulty concept of human nature, and of this the Jeffersonians were the most guilty. It was they who had written equality alone, not equity, into the *Declaration of Independ-*

ence. Equality of citizens "in the eyes of the law," Calhoun of course deemed "essential to liberty in a popular government." The nonvoting citizenry—the Negroes, the women and children—he saw as comparable to the passengers on a ship, not directing the passage, but sharing in the privileges and the protections of the voyage.

To Calhoun equality too often meant only an equal chance for the unequally endowed to compete for a goal. Not equity, but *laissez-faire.* Not protection, but exploitation. And this tragedy had occurred through the Jeffersonians' second faulty concept of human nature. Steeped as they were in the idealism of the French Revolutionary philosophers, they had assumed that an ideal government made ideal men; that the evil in the world was not from men, but from the institutions that held them down. Men were inherently good; and by this fallacy the Jeffersonians had blinded themselves to the danger of unchecked democracy becoming the very source of its own destruction.

For all men were not inherently good, and the institutions that crushed them were themselves man-made. Had the doctrine of inherent goodness been true, then an assumption of equality might have been possible. Recognizing the divine equality of human souls, men of talent would voluntarily have protected, not exploited, those with whom Nature had been less generous.

But the Hamiltonians had understood. Throughout the ages realists of their ilk had perceived the true nature of man. They had understood it and they had exploited it. At seventeen Hamilton had perceived what Calhoun only realized at thirty-seven: that "a vast majority of mankind is entirely biased by motives of self-interest," and that by this interest must be governed.

Bitter experience had opened Calhoun's eyes. Freedom, he knew, was not to be saved by denying the dangers to freedom. An ideal government did not make ideal men. Thomas Jefferson and the French theorists could not do in a generation what Christianity had been unable to do in eighteen hundred years.

Yet where the Hamiltonians, to gratify the aims of the few, would use the facts of human nature to exploit the many, Calhoun would use the same facts to protect all men from one another. If men were selfish, selfishness should be recognized, and when acknowledged, it could be controlled.

Defiant of the French Revolutionary theory of man 'in a state of nature,' Calhoun turned to the facts. Man, he contended, existed only in the social state, and the social state necessitated government. Yet man had "a greater regard for his own safety and happiness than for the safety or happiness of others"; and "hence, the tendency to a universal state of conflict," if not prevented by some controlling power. Government would be completely unnecessary if men truly loved their neighbors as themselves.

Self-interest, Calhoun knew, could be as ruthless in a democracy as in a monarchy. Bitterly he ridiculed "the folly of supposing that the party in possession of the ballot box and the physical force of the country could be successfully resisted by an appeal to reason, truth, justice, or the obligations of the Constitution."

Had not all history taught him otherwise?

What could be done? Calhoun, at least, had an answer. Any political ideal, he contended, was useless, unless built upon a foundation of the facts. And he tore at the facts with a realism that left the last of Jefferson's idealistic concept of men in "shreds and tatters." He re-examined the teachings of the fathers, substituted economic realism for abstract humanitarianism; and based his democratic faith upon a new foundation.

What he proposed was a blending of the two dominant trends of American thought, the Jeffersonian ideal upon the Hamiltonian foundations. Not rejecting majority rule, but expounding it and pro-viding for its control, he worked out a corollary to Jefferson's thought and suggested constitutional reforms that "might prove the salvation of political democracy in America."

His basic solution, the substitution of the "concurrent" for the numerical majority, was revolutionary—perhaps his most revolutionary contribution to political thought. His aim was a government, not "of a part over a part," but of "a part made identical with the whole." How could this be done? By consulting the voice "of each interest or portion of the community, which may be unequally or injuriously affected by the action of the government," before putting laws into operation. "Each division or interest" should have "either a con-current voice in making and executing the laws, or a veto on their execution." Thus would the different interests be "protected, and all conflict and struggle between them prevented."

Calhoun was, of course, sufficiently realistic to know that although in theory he sought "the sense of the entire community," necessarily only "a few great and prominent interests" could be thus represented. Nevertheless, legislation would be more just if enacted by a nation-wide majority of farm, laboring, and financial groups than by a majority of the one over the other.

In a modern application of his plan, the "concurrent veto" seems, of course, the stumbling-block. Yet this objection is lessened if we reject the twentieth-century concept of the term "veto," for which

Calhoun would have had only scorn, and remember that under his nullification theories a state could suspend a law only in relation to itself, not for the rest of the country. And in time of war, Calhoun realized that, Constitution or no Constitution, freedom was at an end, although undoubtedly he would have preferred that the Constitution admit this truth explicitly. His own words were clear: "Government . . . must in the present condition of the world, be clothed with powers sufficient to call forth the resources of the community, and be prepared at all times, to command promptly in all emergencies . . . large establishments . . . both civil and military . . . with well-trained forces in sufficient numbers. . . ." "Liberty must always be subject to power which prevents from internal or external dangers. . . . Liberty must yield to protection; as the existence of the race is of greater moment than its improvement."

18
Louis Hartz: South Carolina vs. the United States[1]

Calhoun's defense of the South as an economic interest represents the same failure of conservatism that we find in his defense of the South as a collection of states. In terms of theory, to be sure, this is not entirely true. When in his political speeches and in the *Disquisition on Government* Calhoun substitutes "minorities" and "interests" for "states" and gives them the power of nullifying national policy, he releases himself from the wild theoretical horse he is trying to ride on the legal plane. Minorities and interests can hardly be called "sovereign," and Calhoun does not call them that. But all that Calhoun really accomplishes by this is to remove his problem from the realm of logic and put it in the realm of social fact. In social fact the Southern minority that Calhoun starts with has been torn away from the rest of the American nation as effectively as the concept of sovereignty would ever tear it away. It is a grim and isolated group, engaged in a war it cannot win, whose secession he actually predicted before he died. Under such circumstances preserving the Union by the simple technique of the "concurrent majority," if not legally illogical, is at any rate practically impossible.

Calhoun's method was to shatter the fabric of American community and then to attempt to restore it by a purely mechanical device. But this was to overlook a very important truth: mechanical devices are only as strong as the sense of community that underlies them. And yet his error was not unprecedented in American thought. The Founding Fathers had made it too. In the minds of many of them, Adams and Hamilton and Morris for example, the American scheme of checks and balances was designed to control a destructive war between proletarians on the one hand and aristocrats on the other. . . . But the case of Calhoun, alas, was somewhat different. The desperate struggle that he was describing was actually becoming a fact. He was making the mistake of the Founding Fathers at the only

[1] From Louis Hartz, "South Carolina vs. the United States," in *America in Crisis*, ed. Daniel Aaron (New York: Alfred A. Knopf, Inc., 1952), pp. 79–83, 88–89.

time in our history when it could readily be exposed. Of course, the "concurrent majority" was not adopted, and neither was his scheme of a dual executive, which embodied it. But if it had been, is it fair to assume that the North would have found it intolerable?

Notice, however, that Calhoun does not merely accept the scheme of Adams: the "concurrent majority" goes beyond it and supplements political checks with economic-interest checks. A threefold division of the functions of government on the national plane is not enough, because a single party can gain control of them simultaneously. Calhoun, in other words, is busily piling up checks in face of the very situation that is going to explode them all. This seems strange but, given the premises of the eighteenth century, is it? Once you concede that mechanical devices can serve as a substitute for the spirit of community which permits them to function, are you not automatically embarked on such a course? There is logic here, even if of a rather inverted kind: the more conflict you have, the more checks you need, and the more certain it is that no checks will work.

*   *   *

But what Calhoun was doing, if he is to be considered a philosopher of our interest-group system, was offering it as a substitute for the social unity on which it rests. Of course, if we were to agree with what he often implies, that the struggle between the North and South were simply the result of using the device of the "numerical majority," there would be nothing fantastic about this procedure. Legislating the log-rolling technique into existence would be a perfectly reasonable act. But the sectional struggle obviously came from deeper sources, as he himself practically admits when he declares the South to be a permanent and hopeless minority. Minorities cannot be permanent unless there is some profound division of interest to make them so. And under such circumstances not even legislation can produce the spirit of pressure-group adjustment. For that spirit is ordinarily possible precisely because the nation is not split into warring social camps, because majorities and minorities are *fluid* and the groups that make them up know that they can easily exchange places on another issue or at another time. Calhoun said that the "concurrent majority" produced the spirit of compromise. What was actually the case, however, was that the spirit of compromise produced the "concurrent majority."

Nothing shows up the anguish of the man more clearly than this perpetual putting of the cart before the horse. . . . The spirit of compromise Calhoun calls for outdoes in amiability even the spirit that pervades a Congressional cloakroom in a time of high profits and high wages. As he himself puts it, each interest will "promote its own prosperity by conciliating the good will, and promoting the prosperity of others." There will be a "rivalry to promote the interests of each other." There will be "patriotism, nationality, harmony, and a struggle only for supremacy in promoting the common good of the whole." All of this when the country is on the brink of civil war, and simply by extending a notch the logic of John Adams! One is tempted to wonder whether the keenest pathos of the compromise spirit before the Civil War lies in the speeches of Henry Clay, or whether it lies right here, in Calhoun, dreaming up out of the South's own bitterness a mirage of social peace the like of which even a peaceful nation has never experienced.

At the time in which Calhoun was writing, however, neither South Carolina nor the South as a whole was quite in the position he made it out to be. There is one problem that Calhoun and other Nullifiers were careful to avoid: the problem of the minority within the minority—the problem, in other words, of the Unionists in South Carolina. It is not strange, given the treatment the Unionists received, that they should blast the Ordinance of Nullification with the very language the Nullifiers used to defend it, that they should call it "the mad edict of a despotic majority." How were the Calhounians to meet this charge? It would have been suicidal for the Nullifiers to give their opponents a veto, but let us suppose, out of passion for logic, that they did. There was also a minority within the Unionist minority, and a minority within that. Were these minorities to be given a veto too? The point I am making is the fairly obvious one that if the minority principle is carried to its logical conclusion it unravels itself out into Locke's state of nature where separate individuals execute the law of nature for themselves. Locke's acceptance of majority rule was by no means ill considered.

But this is merely a logical victory over Calhoun, and it is likely to lead us away from rather than closer to the central problem to be faced. In politics most principles break down when carried to their "logical conclusion," and if a man is brave enough to match his mind against reality, provided he does not use concepts like "sovereignty," which make it impossible, he ought to be given the privilege of silently drawing a few lines. The real significance of the Unionist minority lies in another place. It lies not in the fact that it was a minority but in the fact that it was *Unionist*. And the reason why this is important is that it reveals an important mechanism by which groups are held together in a political community: the mechanism of crisscrossing allegiances. Had the South Carolinians been one hundred per cent in favor of Nullification, or had the Unionist minority simply been indifferent to the question, they would hardly have given up so quickly their challenge to the federal government. But Jackson was in direct negotiation with the Unionist minority—he had promised them all the aid they needed—and this was a very sobering piece of knowledge for the Nullifiers to have. In other words, the fact that South Carolina was not a monolithic entity, as the Calhounian terms of "state" or "interest" or "minority" might imply, had a lot to do with uniting it to the rest of the nation.

If Calhoun's concern with a national "preservative" had transcended everything else, he would have welcomed this empirical defect in his premises. And as a matter of fact, there is a certain amount of evidence, on the wider plane of the struggle between North and South, to suggest that he actually did. With a number of other Southerners, as the Civil War approached, he suggested an alliance between Northern capitalists and Southern planters to keep both the slaves and the free working-class down. This alliance presumably would have helped to save the Union by exploiting common tensions within the sectional interests he usually described in monolithic terms. But Calhoun was in general no philosopher of intrasectional conflict, for the obvious reason that he was too embittered a Southerner. Instead of welcoming this imperfection in his premises, he glossed it over. Which, of course, made it harder than ever for him to reach his conservative conclusions.

History, as usual, was on the side of his premises. The drift toward civil war was a drift toward the consolidation of North and South into increasingly monolithic interests. Intersectional allegiances, one by one, began to disappear. America approached what is probably the most dangerous moment in the political life of any community: the moment of the almost perfect *rationalization* of its internal conflict. This made Calhoun's simplistic antithesis of majority and minority a real one, but what it did for the mechanical approach to politics is a matter of the obvious record. Once again, as in the case of his states'-rights legalism, Calhoun had laid a foundation that exploded the structure he tried to build upon it.

*   *   *

In the perspective of a hundred years of steady centralization the nullification movement has about it a quality as antique as the florid language and the swallowtail coats of the Southern orators who defended it. But if what I have said here is at all correct the antiquity of its significance is superficial enough. Beneath its concern with the sovereign rights of South Carolina and the South lies an issue that is not only permanent but is perhaps the deepest issue that any society, internally or externally, has to face: the issue of law and force, of war and compromise.

Calhoun's approach to this issue was a failure because he started with the premises of force and after that tried to arrive at the conclusions of law. He started with the uncontrollable concept of sovereignty, and then he tried to control it. He started with a condition of the deepest conflict, and then he tried to resolve it with mechanical devices it was bound to destroy. He started with the romantic notion of the divinity and inscrutability of power, and then he tried to erect upon it the rationalism by which it might be limited. He was forever slamming the door in his own face, shutting out the very "preservative" he wanted to create. But how, in the last analysis, are we to judge his effort? We can say the obvious thing: he should have modified his premises, should have laid the basis for law before he attempted to attain it. But Calhoun was a crusader as well as a conservative, which is not necessarily bad. What is a man to do when his honest sense of oppression matches perfectly his love of peace? Here we have one of the mysterious and tragic dilemmas of political life, and because we in our own time have experienced it, we have no right to smile at the agony it caused Calhoun. I do not know what the solution to it is. Perhaps it is right that men should prepare to fight when they find their freedoms at stake, and right also that they should cherish the dream of peace that their preparation destroys.

19

William W. Freehling: Spoilsmen and Interests in the Thought and Career of John C. Calhoun[1]

Calhoun's career spanned the years of transition. Educated at Yale College and the Litchfield Law School at the beginning of the nineteenth century, the South Carolinian studied under Timothy Dwight, James Gould, and Tapping Reeve, three high priests of the Federalist faith. Calhoun remained a Jeffersonian in spite of his mentors. But Jefferson himself prayed that popular majorities would select "natural aristocrats" to govern, and the young Calhoun probably raised few objections to the elitist side of the dogmas handed down at Litchfield and Yale. Calhoun emerged from his encounter with the Federalists steeped in the eighteenth-century conviction that democracies could best survive if enlightened aristocrats continued to rule.

Throughout his ensuing national career Calhoun fought to preserve the Founding Fathers' principles against the onslaught of the emerging political managers. In his brilliant early years as Secretary of War under James Monroe, Calhoun opposed the Presidential aspirations of William H. Crawford partly because the Georgian hoped "to attain favor, not by placing himself on principles and policy . . . but by political dexterity and management."[2] Calhoun's crusade against John Quincy Adams' administration was also partly motivated by growing concern with base political methods. Adams had risen to power, according to Calhoun, by a "corrupt bargain" with Henry Clay in which Adams bought the Presidency by paying Clay with the ap-

[1] From William W. Freehling, "Spoilsmen and Interests in the Thought and Career of John C. Calhoun," *Journal of American History*, LII (June 1965), pp. 25–42. Copyright 1965 by the Organization of American Historians. Reprinted by permission of the editor of *The Journal of American History*.

[2] Calhoun to Charles Fischer, August 1, 1823, Fischer Papers (Southern Historical Collection, University of North Carolina Library).

pointment as Secretary of State.[3] In late 1829, when the political craftiness of Martin Van Buren had begun to drive Calhoun to the rear of the Jackson movement, the South Carolinian wrote John McLean that "I deeply apprehend, that the choice of the chief magistrate will finally be placed at the disposition of the executive power itself, through a corrupt system to be founded on the abuse of the power and patronage of the government." [4]

Thwarted by Van Buren and isolated from Jackson in 1831, Calhoun became a leader of the South Carolina Nullifiers. One of the many reasons for his action was the belief that South Carolina's veto of the tariff would lower governmental revenues and thereby reduce executive patronage.[5] By 1835 the South Carolinian was obsessed with the notion that Jackson's use of the patronage to promote the ascendancy of his own handpicked candidate was turning democracy into dictatorship.[6] Arguing in his "Report on the Extent of the Executive Patronage" that the executive corps was becoming "so strong as to be capable of sustaining itself by the influence alone, unconnected with any system or measure of policy," Calhoun urged Congress to enact controls on "King Andrew's" manipulation of the spoils.[7] Thereafter, in every major policy decision, from distributing the surplus revenue to enacting the Independent Treasury, from lowering the tariff to entering the Mexican War, the "Cast-Iron Man" from South Carolina carefully weighed the effect on executive patronage. For a time, in the late 1830's and early 1840's, Calhoun believed that patronage could be successfully dried up.[8] But by 1848 an embittered Calhoun had almost admitted defeat. He did not see "how any man who has the ability and the disposition to correct abuses and reform the government can in the present state of politics be elected. The governing, I might with truth say, the exclusive object of both parties, in electing the President, is to obtain the spoils. They are both equally ready to sacrifice any other consideration to it." [9]

In denouncing Crawford's use of the Congressional caucus, in casti-

[3] Calhoun to Micah Sterling, August 12, 1827, Calhoun Papers (South Caroliniana Library, Columbia).

[4] Calhoun to John McLean, September 22, 1829, McLean Papers (Manuscript Division, Library of Congress).

[5] Calhoun to the Committee of Arrangements, September 16, 1836, *Pendleton Messenger*, September 30, 1836.

[6] Calhoun to Francis Pickens, May 19, 1835, Calhoun Papers.

[7] Crallé, *Works*, V, 148–190, esp. 163.

[8] Calhoun to Armistead Burt, December 24, 1838, Jameson, *Correspondence*, pp. 422–23.

[9] Calhoun to Elwood Fisher, February 14, 1848, Calhoun Papers.

gating the "corrupt bargain" between Clay and Adams, in thundering against Jackson's distribution of the spoils, Calhoun was not merely echoing the antiparty rhetoric of the Founding Fathers. He was also voicing the typical disdain of a South Carolina patrician for the new political methods in the Age of Jackson. Throughout the first half of the nineteenth century the South Carolina planters remained solidly committed to a quasi-aristocratic version of democracy, and no other group in American society clung more tenaciously to the eighteenth-century ideal of a nation ruled by gentlemen. In his campaign against the spoilsmen, as in so much else, Calhoun can only be understood against the background of the state whose cause he made so peculiarly his own.

The South Carolina patrician was a democrat with the brakes on; he had faith only in the right kind of democracy. If the natural aristocracy was allowed a free hand to govern, the Carolina planter could afford to be a democrat. He conceded that the people should choose which aristocrats would rule. As James Hamilton, Jr., put it, "The people expect that their leaders in whose . . . public spirit they have confidence will think for them—and that they will be prepared to *act* as their leaders *think*." [10]

The South Carolina Constitution of 1790 as amended in the early nineteenth century institutionalized this qualified faith in democracy. Any adult white male who had resided in South Carolina for two years could vote for state legislators. However, the legislators elected almost all other state officials from the Governor to the tax collectors, as well as United States Senators and Presidential electors. A high property qualification for the legislature kept lower-class opportunists outside the statehouse. Finally, the apportionment of legislative seats gave the small minority of low-country aristocrats control of the senate and a disproportionate influence in the house. Political power in South Carolina was uniquely concentrated in a legislature of large property holders which set state policy and selected the men to administer it.[11]

The characteristics of South Carolina politics cemented the control of upper-class planters. Elections to the state legislature—the one control the masses could exert over the government—were often uncontested and rarely allowed the "plebeians" a clear choice between two parties or policies. Even in the state legislature, the Carolina

[10] Hamilton to Stephen Miller, August 9, 1830, Chesnut-Manning-Miller Papers (South Carolina Historical Society, Charleston). See also John Belton O'Neall, *Biographical Sketches of the Bench and Bar of South Carolina*, 2 Vols. (Charleston, 1859), I, 180 ff.; *Edgefield Hive*, April 6, 1830.

[11] J. M. Lesesne, ed., *The Constitution of 1790* (Columbia, 1952).

gentry eschewed organized parties. Leaders of a well-disciplined legislative party might organize a state-wide popular ticket and encourage
the "mob" to overreach themselves by debating issues. Unscrupulous
demagogues would subsequently seize control from disinterested patricians by bribing and deluding the rabble. Political parties would
overturn the rule of the rich, well born, and able, and would thus
upset the precariously balanced, qualified democracy which alone won
the approbation of the South Carolina patricians.[12]

Although sensitive souls throughout the country were disgusted with
the emerging spoils system in the Age of Jackson, the South Carolina
aristocrats shrieked the longest and the loudest. The rise of the political manager upset their delicately balanced, limited democracy and
produced some of the evils they most feared—a passion for federal
patronage, the rule of party hacks, the rise of inferior demagogues.[13]
South Carolina's participation in the political parties was occasional
and superficial. The Calhounites, quickly disillusioned by their bitter
experience with the early Jackson movement, usually remained aloof
from national coalitions. And when Calhoun sporadically and suspiciously rejoined the Democratic party, he always insisted that taxes
should be lowered so that the party would be based on principles
rather than spoils.

However, Calhoun's attempt to reform the Democratic party was
not solely the disinterested campaign of a South Carolina patrician to
reestablish the ideals of the Founding Fathers. His rhetoric on executive patronage also probably reflects the bitter disappointment of a
brilliant and supremely ambitious young man who climbed with in-
credible speed to the higher ranks of federal power and then never
achieved his ultimate goal. Political maneuvering had destroyed his
Presidential prospects of 1832 and threatened to produce a life of
personal frustration. Calhoun may well have realized that his marked

[12] The Carolina statesmen did indulge in extensive public debates during moments of high excitement. However, these political methods were always used with
the most revealing misgivings. For example, during the nullification controversy
the Nullifiers created state-wide political "Associations." But they defended these
political clubs only as an extraordinary response to an unusual crisis and dis-
banded them immediately after the tariff was lowered. The more conservative
unionists feared the demagoguery and corruption of parties so deeply that they
refused to form rival political clubs, and thereby handed the Nullifiers a decisive
advantage. For extended discussion see Freehling, "Nullification Controversy," pp
352–59.

[13] William J. Grayson, the leading planter and proslavery poet, gave classic expression to South Carolina's hatred for the new political brokers in his verdict
on the causes of the Civil War. William J. Grayson, *Autobiography* (typecopy in
South Caroliniana Library), pp. 225–26.

superiority at political reasoning was somewhat offset by his notorious failings as a practical politician. In this sense, he may have hoped that reduced executive patronage would produce a nation where the Calhouns rather than the Van Burens, the philosopher statesman rather than the party managers, would once again have a chance to be President of the United States.[14]

But Calhoun's obsession with political corruption was more than a response to unfulfilled ambition, more than a patrician's distrust of the new political managers. It was also one expression of that violent South Carolina radicalism in the crisis of the 1830's which produced both the nullification crusade against the tariff and the gag rule fight against the abolitionists. The South Carolinians, morbidly aware of their own weaknesses—depressed economically, frightened by recurrent slave conspiracies, able to defend slavery only with the doctrine that bondage was a "necessary evil" (and secretly believing that necessary or not the evil was grave)—found themselves faced for the first time with a mounting abolitionist attack and a high protective tariff, both of which seemed to threaten slavery and the future of Southern white civilization. The planters devised (and tried to believe) a proslavery argument, developed a closed, rigid, restrictive society, and even endeavored (a bit lamely) to acquire some of that Yankee spirit of commercial enterprise which they held in such contempt. But for their ultimate salvation they turned to national policies. Convinced that their only hope lay in the most rigid adherence to principle, the South Carolina aristocrats were made desperate by the apathy of natural allies throughout the nation. Many Southerners seemed content to compromise with the abolitionists. Most Democrats, both North and South, refused to engage in an uncompromising fight against Clay's American System. There could be only one explanation. Politicians were compromising with abolitionists and monopolists to keep their party together and to increase their chances of grabbing a share of the spoils of office. If the American System could be destroyed and patronage reduced, the South might be brought to defend itself in time and

---

[14] This is not to say that Calhoun always shunned the methods he deplored. The South Carolinian enthusiastically directed his own Presidential campaign in the early 1820's, and—as Charles G. Sellers has pointed out to the author—the Calhounites tried to use Van Burenite methods to defeat Van Buren himself in the contest for the Democratic nomination in 1844. But even at such times, Calhoun was somewhat uneasy about using partisan political techniques. See, for example, Calhoun to Duff Green, June 7, 1843, Jameson, *Correspondence*, pp. 537–38. Calhoun's disdain for the new style of democratic politics may have been an important reason for his ineptness as a practical politician. For an illuminating discussion see Gerald M. Capers, *John C. Calhoun—Opportunist* (Gainesville, 1960).

the Democrats brought to stand steadfast on the only principles which
could save the union.[15] And surely Calhoun's belief that politicians
often ignore their constituents in their race for the spoils originated
in part with what he considered the shame of the spoilsmen in the
1830's.

Thus, in his practical career as in his political theory, Calhoun's
concern with spoilsmen was as important as his fear of interests. By
exorcising the new political brokers Calhoun could hope to bring the
Republic back to the enlightened rule of disinterested patricians, fulfill his Presidential ambitions, and develop national political movements based on principles rather than spoils. When statesmen replaced
spoilsmen, the clash between fundamental interests over the American
System and over abolition could also be resolved.

Yet Calhoun's practical program was vitiated by the same logical
contradiction between the theory of interests and the theory of spoilsmen which destroyed his political philosophy. The South Carolinian
was again unable to decide whether pressure groups or politicians
caused historical events. On the one hand, Calhoun held that the
Democratic party would be run by spoilsmen rather than statesmen
until the American System ceased to supply patronage. On the other
hand, he maintained that the American System would only be destroyed when statesmen replaced spoilsmen at the head of the Democratic party. If interests could be neutralized, spoilsmen would disappear. Yet spoilsmen must disappear before interests could be
neutralized. The reformer hardly knew where to begin. As Calhoun
saw the dilemma in a more practical situation, Jackson's Democratic
politicos—although elected by interest groups opposed to Clay's
brainchild—compromised with an American System which fed them
patronage, thereby frustrating their constituents.

Nullification was, among other things, a desperate way out of the
vicious circle. South Carolina, by nullifying high duties, could at once
neutralize interests and reduce patronage. For a time in the late 1830's
Calhoun was almost sanguine. But even nullification was no real
escape, for by Calhoun's own admission the unnullified military
establishments remained to invite the resurgence of spoilsmen. More
important, in the 1840's, with nullification discredited, the South
Carolinian was again trapped in his own logical nightmare. Thus
when Democrats like Thomas Ritchie and Van Buren compromised
a bit with the American System and with the abolitionists, Calhoun's

[15] Crallé, *Works*, I, 375; Calhoun to James Hammond, January 25, April 2, 1840;
Calhoun to Thomas G. Clemson, June 7, 1845, Jameson, *Correspondence*, pp. 443,
452, 663–64.

profound bitterness was the logical culmination of the inconsistencies in his own political program.

The *Disquisition,* written in the late 1840's, reflects Calhoun's despair as his career drew to a close. The increasingly angry controversy between Northern and Southern interests seemed disastrous enough in itself. But in addition the vast federal patronage seemed certain to perpetuate the regime of the spoilsmen. With unscrupulous politicians in power the North and South would never find grounds for reconciliation. Thus the *Disquisition* represents one of Calhoun's last desperate attempts to restrain the interests and spoilsmen which together seemed destined to break up the republic.

In one sense, the *Disquisition* is a justly celebrated contribution to the American democratic tradition. Calhoun was a political realist who ranks with James Madison and John Adams in his mordant analysis of the defects of a democracy. As Calhoun endlessly reiterated, entrenched majorities can ignore constitutional restraints and pay little heed to minority rights. The South Carolinian was also clearly right that the clash of interests and the intrigues of spoilsmen often threaten the efficiency of a democratic government.

The problem with the *Disquisition* lies not in its diagnosis but rather in its exaggeration of the weaknesses in a republic. Calhoun's critics have often argued that the theory of interests overstates both the helplessness of democratic minorities and the selfishness of economic interests. It must now be added that the theory of spoilsmen magnifies the threat posed by scheming politicians. Ambitious demagogues may sometimes exert more political influence than the economic determinists like to think. But Calhoun surely overestimated the spoilsmen's capacity to delude the masses and overthrow the system. Indeed Calhoun's rhetoric on the evils of patronage often sounds suspiciously like that of a late nineteenth-century mugwump, fighting his curious crusade to save democracy by enacting civil service reform. The combination of this exaggerated fear of spoilsmen and Calhoun's exaggerated fear of interests simply posed problems too grave for the concurrent majority, or any constitutional reform, to solve. The resulting inconsistencies in the *Disquisition* must create renewed doubts as to whether Calhoun deserves his reputation as America's most rigorous political logician. It would be closer to the truth to call the author of the *Disquisition* one of the more confused political philosophers in the American tradition.[16]

[16] Louis Hartz reaches a similar conclusion from a different direction in his brilliant comments on Calhoun. See Hartz, *The Liberal Tradition in America* (New York, 1955), pp. 145–77.

The contradictions in Calhoun's *Disquisition* provide a particularly revealing illustration of that ambivalence toward democratic principles which so often marked the political thought of the more aristocratic Southern slaveholders. As historians have often reminded us in the past two decades, the clash between American politicians has characteristically taken place within a consensus of belief in democratic government. Calhoun paid his personal testimonial to this pervasive American consensus by straining to remain both a statesman and a theorizer of the democratic persuasion. But the deeper significance of Calhoun's tragic career is that despite his fascination with abstract political argument he could not put together a consistent democratic theory. The key to Calhoun's thought is not just his concern with class or any other kind of economic interests, not just his concern with moral fanatics, not just his concern with demagogic spoilsmen. Rather, the secret of his political philosophy—the reason why it is inevitably inconsistent—is that Calhoun distrusted democracy for so many exaggerated and contradictory reasons. An eighteenth-century elitist increasingly disillusioned with the emerging political order in the Age of Jackson, Calhoun by the end of his career no longer quite believed in American democracy.

Afterword and Some Notes on Further Reading

"Patriot or destroyer of the Union?" queries the cover-jacket of John C. Calhoun's most recent biography, Richard Current's provocative attempt to revise the revisionists.[1] Twentieth-century historical estimates of Calhoun range all the way from William Dodd's melancholy conclusion that "no group of public men proclaim allegiance to [Calhoun's] doctrines," to Peter Drucker's assertation that "it is consequently, not that Calhoun was repudiated by the Civil War, which is the key to the understanding of American politics, but that he has become triumphant since." Current asserts that indeed a significant group does claim him as spokesman, the segregationists and states' rights Dixiecrats; biographer Charles M. Wiltse contends that "he spoke for all minorities in all democratic states."

Calhoun has always commanded the admiration of his fellow Senators, and, in particular, of Senators from Massachusetts, the opposite pole to South Carolina. Among his contemporaries, the man who admired him most, as we have seen, was the Senator most closely matched to him intellectually, Daniel Webster. Half a century later, upon the placing of the Calhoun monument in Statuary Hall, another brilliant Massachusetts Senator and scholar, Henry Cabot Lodge, paid tribute to Calhoun's "remarkable powers," and wished only that he could stand with his peers around him, "not elbowed and crowded by the temporarily notorious and the illustrious obscure. His statue is here of right. . . . He was one of the most remarkable men, one of the keenest minds that American public life can show. It matters not that before the last tribunal, the verdict went against him . . . the man remains greatly placed in our history." [2]

Again half a century passed and again a Senator-scholar from Massachusetts rose to recognize Calhoun as "the most notable political thinker ever to sit in the Senate, whose doctrine of concurrent majorities has permanently influenced our political theory and practice." John F. Kennedy echoed Lodge in saying that the "ultimate tragedy" of Calhoun's final cause "neither detracts from the greatness of his

---

[1] Richard M. Current, *John C. Calhoun* (New York, 1966).
[2] Henry Cabot Lodge, *The Democracy of the Constitution* (New York: Charles Scribner's Sons, 1915), pp. 165–66, 184–85.

165

leadership nor tarnishes his efforts to avoid bloodshed." [3] Kennedy spoke as chairman of a special Senate committee to select the five outstanding Senators of the past. Calhoun was chosen by the advisory panel of 150 scholars and by the Senators themselves. Although his peers have judged him to be one of the greatest Senators of all time, Calhoun has yet to join such fellow immortals as Phineas T. Barnum and Louisa Alcott in the American Hall of Fame.

A stormcenter in his lifetime, the great South Carolinian has remained a figure of controversy ever since his death. Through two centuries, his very name has come to symbolize the passions aroused by the Negro question, whether in terms of slavery or freedom. This is his relevance. Aside from his political theory and its insights into the working of the American constitutional system, Calhoun more than any other American historical figure is identified with the question of race and its significance in our history. Despite Current's assertion that Calhoun tried to make states' rights a bulwark against human rights, he was not a racist as we understand the term today. He hated no one and no group. He saw the black man as culturally different, not necessarily inferior. If the slave could not vote in his time, neither could the propertyless nor women, all of whom were, in a sense, subject citizens.

He was tragically, fatally wrong in his belief that there was no alternative for slavery or that it was a sound basis for free institutions. He was tragically, fatally right in his belief that the threat of enforced emancipation would bring misery and civil war, drench the country in blood, and forge a temporary alliance between the Northern whites and Southern blacks who would only be cast aside when no longer needed. He knew that what the North was interested in was the slave, what the South was concerned with was the Negro, and that aside from its desire for emancipation, the North had made no plans whatever for the integration of the freed man into the white Northern society. Nor were plans made until population shifts brought "the Negro problem" northward, a century after Calhoun's time. And knowing human nature as he did, knowing how little, in the long run, men either love or help their fellow man, Calhoun foresaw the ultimate outcome of the problem much as we know it today. Society would be divided into two classes: tax payers and tax consumers, the affluent and the poor; and those who had been the slaves of individuals would become, in effect, wards of the community or the government. Calhoun did not analyze why this should be so—the dependency en-

[3] U.S., Congress, Senate, *Congressional Record*, 85th Cong., 1st sess., May 1, 1957, 103, pt. 5:6026.

gendered by the slave system, the matriarchal family patterns, the effects of white prejudice in engendering feelings and, consequently, behavior in terms of inferiority, the possibility of genetic inequities— a question Jefferson had pondered. But he was convinced that "the differences" were there, seemingly too great to be surmounted.

It is possible to surmise that Calhoun's puritanical concept of the doctrine of God's Elect colored his view of the slavery question. Sub-consciously, he may even have seen the masters as "the Elect" and the slaves as those predestined to be damned. If this was the product of his grim Calvinist-Presbyterian upbringing, so, too, was his concept of man's inherent evil—selfishness Calhoun called it—which rendered government necessary. If men truly loved their neighbors, if it was not in their nature to exploit, rather than to aid their fellow men, there would be no need for government. But because each man looked first to himself, government itself could become corrupt and was thus sub-ject to some check or controlling power.

Not for Calhoun the comfortable doctrines of the Enlightenment or the French Revolution. He brushed aside contemptuously the view that man was born innocent in a state of nature and corrupted only by the corruption of the society around him. Ever the realist, Calhoun knew that men were not born free or equal or apart from the society into which they came. He was convinced that man made his own corruption. Calhoun's own fatalistic belief that he moved according to destiny reflected the working of this grim philosophy within him.

But Calhoun was not only a Calvinist; his world was a Newtonian, mechanistic universe that reflected with mathematical precision the forethought and planning of God. It was a world that had been shaped and set in motion by the Master Builder, an ordered world in an ordered universe of scientific certainties.

Calhoun's was never a Rousseauist world. He scorned the Enlighten-ment, as he scorned both the concepts of progress and perfectibility. He was pre-Darwinian and foreshadowed Marx. His pre-Marxist evalua-tion of the class struggle, a struggle which, as we have seen, he not only foresaw, but strove to repress, seems refreshingly realistic and modern. Calhoun might, therefore, be called a man of three worlds: the Cal-vinist, the Newtonian, and the pre-Marxist, and it is this complexity which makes him so interesting today.

In his own time, Calhoun was generally regarded as a brilliant statesman and dedicated patriot, except by those who saw his slavery and nullification theories as incendiary. The Civil War, which he had so somberly predicted, brought a revulsion of feeling against him. Many viewed him as the evil genius of the conflict, the incarnation of the slave interests who had precipitated the disaster. Visiting Calhoun's tomb in 1865, William Lloyd Garrison struck it with his hand. "Down into a deeper grave than this," he said, "has slavery gone."

Calhoun was not written out of the history books in the latter part of the nineteenth century. His name, in fact, glowed with a "lurid intensity," his biographer von Holst noted, as the symbol of a lost and discredited cause. None imagined that he had anything to say to times beyond his own; none dreamed that he might be rediscovered as a statesman-philosopher of national as well as sectional importance.

In 1900 all the Calhoun letters then available were published in *The Annual Report of the American Historical Association* for the previous year. The flood tide began. During the next seventy-odd years, Calhoun was the subject of seven biographies, including one massive three-volume study and one winner of the Pulitzer Prize. His political theory was given two book-length treatments, and three volumes discussed South Carolina, Calhoun, and the doctrine of nullification. Essays on the man and his ideas have been written by some of the foremost writers of our time: Vernon Parrington, William Trent, Hamilton Basso, Herbert Agar, Ralph Gabriel, Richard Hofstadter, and Louis Hartz, among others. Scholars like Charles M. Wiltse, Ralph Lerner, Peter Drucker, and Richard Current wrote critiques for the scholarly journals; more popular appraisals appeared in magazines of mass circulation like *Harper's, The Atlantic, Time, The Saturday Evening Post,* and *The New York Times Magazine.*

In 1959, the University of South Carolina began the most massive Calhoun project yet undertaken, the publication of his complete correspondence, speeches, and works, a project which will encompass years and produce at least fifteen volumes. In 1952, a collection of Calhoun's *Basic Documents* had appeared,[4] and in 1968, *A Profile,* comprised of a dozen nineteenth- and twentieth-century essays was published.[5] Calhoun has experienced not only a rediscovery, but a virtual resurrection.

From 1925 into the 1950's, much of the Calhoun literature was revisionist in nature. It strove to reevaluate Calhoun as a national, rather than a sectional figure; it integrated his philosophy into the mainstream of the American political tradition and depicted him as a political scientist with unique insights into the workings of the American democratic processes. In my own biography of Calhoun, *John C. Calhoun: American Portrait,* I summarized this view: "Judged by

[4] John M. Anderson, ed., *Calhoun: Basic Documents* (State College, Pa., 1952).
[5] John L. Thomas, ed., *John C. Calhoun: A Profile* (New York, 1968).

ater times and his meaning for them, Calhoun stands in the first
ank of men America has produced. For as a thinker and prophet, he
vas more important for later times than for his own."

British historian Christopher Hollis ranks Calhoun among the first
our American statesmen. "He was wrong," wrote Arthur Schlesinger,
[r., "but he was a greater man and Senator than many people who
iave been right." [6] Another Pulitzer Prize-winning historian, Allan
Nevins, declared that Calhoun "made the most original and profound
:ontributions to constitutional theory. His doctrine that a concurrent
najority is much to be preferred in government to an absolute major-
ty still has force. It was his great object, he said, to require the parts of
American society to be just to each other by compelling them to con-
.ult the interests of each other. He wished a harmonious Union." [7]

This then was the view of the so-called neo-Calhounites. It was a
riew countered by scholars like Richard Hofstadter and Richard
Current who, at best, saw Calhoun as a prophet of reaction, and at
vorst as an enemy of human rights and of the Union as the guardian
)f human rights. Other scholars, writing in the 1950's and 1960's were
;uardedly critical, taking a position midway between the extremes of
hese two groups.

Herbert Agar, in his Pulitzer Prize-winning book, *The Pursuit of
Happiness*, applied Calhoun's theory to the conflicts between economic
;roups in our own time. William W. Freehling's study, *Prelude to
Civil War*, presented a full-scale treatment of "The Nullification Con-
roversy in South Carolina." Freehling interpreted nullification against
ts complex backgrounds: the Lockean social contract theory, Black-
.tone's theory of sovereignty, and the codepartment theorists of the
Constitution. In the end, Freehling exposed "the fatal contradiction
n Calhoun's theory of sovereignty," with a logical analysis that would
iave delighted Calhoun were he able to argue it. But Freehling saw
Calhoun as a devoted Unionist, not the mere symbol of the Lost
Cause; it was love of the Union that entangled him in his "snarl of
:ontradictions."

Calhoun books that have appeared during the 1960's include *John
C. Calhoun: Opportunist,* a short, critical biography by Gerald Capers.
His realistic appraisal interprets Calhoun as in large part motivated
by ambition. Richard Current's *John C. Calhoun* in the Great American Thinkers Series is not so much a biography as an analysis and

[6] Arthur M. Schlesinger, Jr., *The Age of Jackson* (Boston and New York, 1945),
p. 405.
[7] U.S., Congress, Senate, *Congressional Record*, 85th Cong., 1st sess., May 1, 1957,
103, pt. 5:6028.

critique of Calhoun's philosophy. His penetrating study of Calhoun's theories is married by a moral bias; in essence, Current sees Calhoun as primarily a special pleader for the slaveholders. In the wake of the Civil Rights movement, judgments of Calhoun have come full circle.

What matters is that the man is so startlingly alive today. Curiously archaic, strangely modern, he was a nationalist who made a sacred cause out of states' rights, a legalist who saw the law primarily as a defense against majorities, a liberal who called for the abolition of the electoral college and for the citizens to vote directly for President and Vice-President, and a reactionary who saw slavery as the soundest foundation for liberty. But always he dealt with fundamentals. The primary concern of his life was not, in essence, states' rights or slavery or disunion, but the enduring problem of how to preserve liberty for the parts and still maintain power in the whole, how to give the different segments of society, "labor, capital, and production," each the means of self-protection. "Let it never be forgotten," he warned, "that power can only be opposed by power . . . on this theory stands our . . . federal system."

Calhoun died aware that all he had fought for, the South and the Union, would be lost. He had battled the spirit of the age and this was his tragedy. It is no accident that he attracted the lightning. Storms crashed about him during his lifetime and after it, and the final word has yet to be written. His ultimate meaning is yet to be assessed, his place in our history precisely defined. So powerful and creative was his intellect, so complex his personality, so blind his vision on one subject and so far-sighted on so much else, so impressive his attempts to lay "a solid foundation for political science," that we may expect the man and his philosophy to remain storm centers of controversy for many years to come.

Index

GREAT LIVES OBSERVED

Gerald Emanuel Stearn, *General Editor*

Other volumes in the series: